Automation and Alienation

A Study of Office and Factory Workers

The MIT Press Cambridge, Massachusetts, and London, England

Automation and Alienation

A Study of Office and Factory Workers

Jon M. Shepard

To Kay

Contents

Foreword by Charles A. Myers   ix

Acknowledgments   xi

1 The Impact of Technology on Work   1

2 Dimensions of Alienation and Research Methods   13

3 Technology and Alienation: Industrial Workers   23

4 The Changing Nature of Office Work   41

5 Technology and Alienation: Office Employees   63

6 Comparison of Office and Factory Workers   96

7 Mechanization, Automation, and Alienation in the Factory and Office: An Overview   107

Appendix A Scale Construction   129

Appendix B Distinction between Mechanization and Automation   136

Bibliography   145

Index   157

Foreword

The impact of technology on workers has concerned
social scientists, managers, and labor leaders since the
Industrial Revolution. Automation — the modern
dimension of technological change — has conjured
in many minds the spector of the automatic factory or
the computerized office, with labor displacement and
a deadening routine of work.

This important study puts to rest extreme fears about
the alienation of workers as a consequence of automation.
Professor Shepard's study provides new insights about
the impact of advanced mechanization and automation
in offices, which computers and allied information
technology are invading at a rapid rate.

The field work for the office part of the study was
completed during 1968–1969 in Boston, when Professor
Shepard was a full-time Research Associate in the
Industrial Relations Section of the Alfred P. Sloan
School of Management at M.I.T. He drew on his previous
research in factories to develop hypotheses that he then
tested in office jobs in five insurance companies and one
large bank. His research was supported under a grant
by the Ford Foundation to the Sloan School for studies
of organizational behavior. A supplementary grant for
summer work was made by the Office of Manpower
Research in the Manpower Administration of the
U.S. Department of Labor.

This book is one of the last in a series of research
studies of the impact of computers completed by the
Industrial Relations Section. As a sociologist among
economists, Professor Shepard has brought fresh perspective to this series of research reports.

Charles A. Myers

July 1970

Acknowledgments

Adequate thanks cannot be given to the officers and members of the local union who opened their membership files in order that samples could be drawn. Management of the oil refinery could not have been more helpful, permitting, as they did, interviews to be conducted on the job. Likewise, the managements of the five insurance companies and the bank opened for study the desired units of their organizations. Of course, without the cooperation of the many employees of all these companies, the research could have never been completed.

I wish to thank Dean William Pounds of the Sloan School of Management and Charles A. Myers, Director of the Industrial Relations Section of the Sloan School, for the opportunity to conduct the white-collar segment of the study. Both Professor Myers and Douglass V. Brown, also of the Industrial Relations Section, provided counsel and encouragement. Professor Myers spent many hours editing the manuscript and contributed unnumbered improvements. The contribution of Seeni Murthy, my research assistant at M.I.T., who spent untold hours "communicating" with the computer, cannot be overestimated.

I wish to express gratitude to the University of Kentucky which granted me, under unusual circumstances, a leave of absence for the year spent at M.I.T.

All books have a history longer than the actual period of investigation. The antecedents of this volume are found in my years of graduate study at Michigan State University. Appreciation far beyond the present context is extended to William H. Form, William A. Faunce, and Einar Hardin. Special thanks are due Professor Hardin for his critical reading of the manuscript.

A special place is reserved for my wife, Kay, and son, Jon, who often had to settle for less of my time than they deserved.

Appreciation is due the Office of Manpower Research in the Manpower Administration of the U.S. Department of Labor for supporting the entire blue-collar phase of the project and providing funds for much of the final writing. Equal appreciation is due the Ford Foundation which supported the white-collar phase through the Industrial Relations Section of the Sloan School of Management at M.I.T.

Mrs. Linda Holt deserves credit far beyond the ordinary for her efforts in typing and proofreading the manuscript in each of its phases.

Finally, one cannot read this book without recognizing the extent to which it is predicated on the prior work of Robert Blauner and William Faunce.

Jon M. Shepard

July 1970

1 The Impact of Technology on Work

Historically in the factory, and more recently in the office, the predominant philosophy holds that specialization of function is the most desirable form of work arrangement.[1] This philosophy in job design is based on the conviction that specialization of function leads to the greatest efficiency and economy. Accompanying these assumed benefits of functional specialization, however, has been the appearance of some unsalutary social psychological effects in workers.

It was especially the young Karl Marx who saw meaning in productive labor as the "first necessity in life." Man's inherent potentialities, contended Marx, remain unfulfilled when he cannot engage in creative effort. Loss of intrinsic involvement in work, or *self-estrangement*, follows the "objectification" of labor brought about by capitalistic economic institutions, the factory system of production and minute division of labor. Though in different ideological cloaks, many others have shared this concern for the quality of the workingman's experience while earning his living. These critics deplore the historical trend toward higher levels of differentiation in the division of labor at work, contending that a loss of meaning in work has been a significant negative consequence of mass-production techniques.[2] That their concern is not without founda-

1. Extreme specialization of function denotes a minute subdivision of tasks such that each worker is assigned to perform one or a few small operations out of the total production process. Throughout this book functional specialization, minute subdivision of labor, and a high degree of differentiation in the division of labor are used interchangeably.
2. Daniel Bell, "Adjusting Men to Machines," *Commentary*, 3 (January 1947), pp. 79–88; and Harvey Swados, "The Myth of the Happy Worker," *Man Alone: Alienation in Modern Society,*

tion is evident in much social science research. Investigations conducted among blue-collar workers employed in mechanized work settings point to functional specialization as a contributor to negative attitudes toward work.[3] Friedmann,[4] presenting evidence that beyond some point functional specialization has diminishing returns, contends that both management and social scientists are becoming aware of this fact.

Another factor representing a trend away from functional specialization is automation, heralded as a form of production technology that will return to the worker the meaning in work that mechanization seems to preclude. It has recently been argued[5] that automated technology represents a dramatic change in production technology that is characterized by a less specialized division of labor. And research done in both semi-automated (transfer technology or "Detroit" automation) and automated (continuous-process) work settings

Eric Josephson and Mary Josephson, eds. (New York: Dell, 1962), pp. 106–113.
3. Charles R. Walker and Robert H. Guest, *The Man on the Assembly Line* (Cambridge: Harvard University Press, 1952); Charles R. Walker, "The Problem of the Repetitive Job," *Harvard Business Review*, 28 (May 1950), pp. 54–58; J. Walker and R. Marriott, "A Study of Some Attitudes to Factory Work," *Occupational Psychology*, 25 (July 1951), pp. 181–191; Ely Chinoy, *Automobile Workers and the American Dream* (Garden City, New York: Doubleday & Company, Inc., 1955); Robert Blauner, *Alienation and Freedom* (Chicago: University of Chicago Press, 1964); and Louis E. Davis, "The Design of Jobs," *Industrial Relations*, 6 (October 1966), pp. 21–45.
4. Georges Friedmann, *The Anatomy of Work* (Glencoe, Illinois: The Free Press, 1961).
5. Robert Blauner, *Alienation and Freedom;* and William A. Faunce, "Automation and the Division of Labor," *Social Problems,* 13 (Fall 1965), pp. 149–160.

reveals improved attitudes toward work among production personnel.[6]

While there is an abundance of research on the relationship between technology, job specialization, and work attitudes among factory workers, one must conduct a much more diligent search in the case of office employees.[7] This lack of research is understandable since advanced mechanization and automation in the office are relatively recent phenomena. However, two trends in the white-collar world of work render this situation intolerable. First, computers and allied information technology are being introduced into offices at an accelerating rate. During World War II, electronic computers were developed and used for solving scientific and engineering problems. Their use in the office began in 1951 when the federal government employed an electronic computer in the compilation of the 1950 Census of Population. In 1954, the first computer installation in a business organization was completed.

---

6. Charles R. Walker, *Toward the Automatic Factory* (New Haven: Yale University Press, 1957); William A. Faunce, "Automation in the Automobile Industry: Some Consequences for In-Plant Social Structures," *American Sociological Review,* 23 (August 1958), pp. 401–409; Floyd C. Mann and Richard L. Hoffman, *Automation and the Worker* (New York: Henry Holt, 1960); and Blauner, *Alienation and Freedom.*

7. J. Douglas Elliott, "Increasing Office Productivity Through Job Enlargement," in *The Human Side of the Office Manager's Job,* No. 134, Office Management Series (New York: American Management Association, 1953), pp. 3–15; Robert H. Guest, "Job Enlargement—A Revolution in Job Design," *Personnel Administration,* 20 (March–April 1957), pp. 9–16; Floyd C. Mann and Lawrence K. Williams, "Observations on the Dynamics of a Change to Electronic Data Processing Equipment," *Administrative Science Quarterly,* 5 (September 1960), pp. 217–256; and Ida R. Hoos, "When the Computer Takes Over the Office," *Harvard Business Review,* 38 (July–August 1960), pp. 102–112.

The proliferation of computers in offices has been remarkably rapid since then. For example, in 1954 there were two insurance companies with computers. As of 1964, there were nearly 700 computers operating in 226 insurance companies. The number of electronic computers in use in the federal government has sky-rocketed from three in 1951 to an estimated 2,451 in 1966.[8] A 1966 estimate for all industries puts the total number of computer installations in the United States in the neighborhood of 30,000.[9] A recent article in *The New York Times* placed the number of computers now installed in the United States at 56,000; an IBM advertisement claims the number of computers in use to be 60,000.[10]

Second, the gap between the proportion of the American labor force engaged in white-collar occupations compared to the percentage employed in the blue-collar sector is widening. Both of these trends are recent and make the study of the impact of technology on office work and office employee attitudes imperative.

C. Wright Mills[11] makes much of the idea that the modern office, due to technology and rationalization of work, increasingly takes on the character of the factory. This contention, though not without impressionistic support, may be misleading because of the assump-

---

8. U.S. Department of Labor, Bureau of Labor Statistics Bulletin Number 1474, *Technological Trends in Major American Industries* (Washington, D.C.: U.S. Government Printing Office, 1966), pp. 251, 257.
9. "On-Site Systems Top 30,000 Mark," *Business Automation,* 13 (February 1966), pp. 54–56.
10. It should not be overlooked that these are second- and third-generation computers, which are infinitely more advanced in capability than first-generation computers introduced in the 1950s.
11. C. Wright Mills, *White Collar* (New York: Oxford University Press, 1956), pp. 224ff.

tion of homogeneity in office work. Recent research demonstrates the possibility of error in such an assumption. Blauner[12] marshals evidence that automated technology returns to the factory worker the freedom and control, purpose and function, and self-involvement in work that mechanization has taken away. Alienation, according to Blauner, is lower among workers in industries with craft and automated technologies than among workers in mass production or mechanized industries. The utility of examining different man-machine relationships among nonsupervisory office employees is a lesson to be learned from this research among factory workers.

That the introduction of a computerized system in the office portends change is not debatable. Work environment, employee attitudes toward work, and the degree of occupational specialization are all expected to undergo modification. However, drawing diametric conclusions, one researcher may report unfavorable employee reactions to the introduction of electronic data-processing technology while another reports increased employee satisfaction after computerization. An important factor, the level of technological development, may help to account for some of these conflicting results. Differentiation between mechanization and automation in the office is often obscured by assuming that they are identical.[13] The term "office automation" has been used without respect to differences among the several man-machine relationships existing in a computerized business organization. Filling this gap is important because such an undifferentiated view may conceal variations in the impact of technology on work attitudes of office personnel.

---

12. Blauner, *Alienation and Freedom.*
13. For a discussion of the definition of automation see Appendix B.

There is reason to believe that among clerical employees technologically induced changes in the division of labor create man-machine relationships analogous to those in the factory.[14] It is important to know if mechanization and automation in the office have an effect on white-collar employees similar to that documented by Blauner for factory workers. Consequently, while one chapter is devoted to alienation among factory workers, the main emphasis in this book is on technology and alienation in the office. As a second unique feature, data are presented that compare levels and types of alienation among office and factory workers.

TECHNOLOGY AND FUNCTIONAL SPECIALIZATION
If the extent of differentiation in the division of labor contributes to work attitudes among factory workers, it constitutes an important dimension around which to center a study of office employees. What follows is a framework developed on blue-collar work, which can be applied to the contemporary office as well.[15]

Faunce[16] associates a characteristic form of division of labor with each of three stages in the application of technology to industrial production. This association

---

14. This point is pursued in detail in Chapter 4.
15. An important assumption is that the type of technology employed in a production system is normally a major determinant of the manner in which labor is divided. This is not necessarily the case, only the current norm. Job enlargement and job-rotation programs attest that tasks can be assigned differently under a mechanized mode of production.
   An equally crucial presupposition is that the manner in which labor is divided determines a number of other job characteristics. To illustrate, extreme functional specialization creates a job that is repetitive, requires scant skill, and permits no discretion in the selection of tools and procedures.
16. Faunce, "Automation and the Division of Labor."

is due to the presence of a unique man-machine relationship attending each type of production technology. These man-machine relationships represent varying degrees of differentiation in the division of labor at work.

Most workers in *craft production systems* are skilled artisans. The division of labor is not highly differentiated because workers either fashion the total product from raw materials or make substantial contributions to a product.

In *mechanized production systems* many workers become special-purpose machine operators laboring under a high degree of job specialization. The worker who makes only a minute contribution to a product as it comes to his work station on a conveyor is the prototype, but factory machine operators of all kinds also represent this man-machine relationship. Walker and Guest in their classic study of the automobile assembly line enumerate six characteristics of the average mass production job: mechanical pacing of work, repetitiveness, minimum skill requirements, predetermination in the use of tools and techniques, surface mental attention, and minute subdivision of labor. From their discussion it is apparent that the primary factor, of which most of the other characteristics appear to be consequences, is the minute subdivision of labor.[17]

Another fundamental change in the man-machine relationship is contained in *automated production systems*. The operator in a continuous-process plant is a monitor of an integrated production system. Essentially, he makes periodic readings on instruments that relay information on whether the production process is functioning normally. Automation produces job enlargement in the sense that control room operators are

---

17. Walker and Guest, *The Man on the Assembly Line,* p. 12.

responsible for a larger share of the production process as the number of job classifications are reduced. Job enlargement occurs as formerly discrete steps in the production process are integrated. Integration of functions eliminates some job classifications. Remaining operating jobs are enlarged, comprised as they are of several combined functions which prior to automation were performed by separate operators. Automation from this perspective reverses the trend toward functional specialization in industrial manufacturing.[18]

The argument is developed in Chapter 4 that technologically induced changes in the division of labor create man-machine relationships among nonsupervisory clerical employees similar to those in manufacturing. Sufficient for the present is a summary of this analogy. The nonmechanized production stage in the office contains two general types of clerical employees: those who do not use machines in the course of their work (clerks of all kinds) and employees who utilize simple machines as adjuncts to the performance of work tasks

---

18. Several pieces of research suggest that automated technology results in a diminution in separate job classifications. These studies are cited in Faunce, "Automation and the Division of Labor," p. 156. In order of mention they are U.S. Department of Labor, Bureau of Labor Statistics, *A Case Study of a Large Mechanized Bakery* (Washington, D.C.: U.S. Government Printing Office, 1956), p. 16; Walker, *Toward the Automatic Factory,* p. 61; and Mann and Hoffman, *Automation and the Worker,* p. 72.

A number of studies permit the conclusion that job enlargement—responsibility for a larger span of the production process—is a concomitant of automation. See Faunce, "Automation in the Automobile Industry"; James R. Bright, *Automation and Management* (Boston: Division of Research, Graduate School of Business Administration, Harvard University, 1958); Blauner, *Alienation and Freedom;* and Mann and Hoffman, *Automation and the Worker.*

(for example, secretaries using typewriters). Office employees characterized by this man-machine relationship normally perform a number of manual tasks such as filing, typing, and recording. The punched-card system of data processing requires operators for special-purpose machines such as key-punchers, tabulators, sorters, and printers. This stage of office mechanization is not unlike the mechanized production system characteristic of the modern factory. With the development of more complex computers for business application, new man-machine relationships are created. The computer-console operator functions in a fashion paralleling monitors in continuous-process manufacturing industries. Console operators experience job enlargement in the sense that they are responsible for a large share of a partially integrated information-processing system. Computer software personnel (programmers and systems analysts) represent another new man-machine relationship created by the application of computers to data processing.

OVERVIEW

The following question is explored in this study: Does a worker's relationship to technology and division of labor at work influence in a predictable way his integration into or alienation from work? It will be shown for both the office and factory that the degree of differentiation in the division of labor at work is related to technology and that automated technology reduces the levels of alienation among office employees as well as among factory workers.

It is assumed that there is a curvilinear relationship between the phases in the man-machine relationship and the degree of differentiation in the division of labor: nonmechanized production—lower differentiation; mechanized production—higher differentiation; au-

tomated production—lower differentiation.[19] Against
the background in this chapter the hypothesis can be
stated that there is a curvilinear relationship between
the phases in the man-machine relationship and worker
alienation: nonmechanized production—lower alienation; mechanized production—higher alienation;
automated production—lower alienation. This hypothesis will be tested by sampling within each of these
three man-machine relationships among white-collar
employees and blue-collar workers.[20] The predicted
relationships between the phases in the man-machine
relationship, division of labor, and alienation from
work, along with the types of office and factory workers
sampled for each man-machine relationship, are presented in Table 1.1.

There are two essential ways in which the results ob-

---

19. The prediction of curvilinear relationships is based on con-
ceiving the three man-machine relationships as historical stages
in the development of technology (from nonmechanization to
mechanization to automation). While all three types of production systems exist simultaneously today, they still represent stages
in the development of technology as applied to industrial manufacturing and data processing in the office.
20. Any production system, whatever the technology, contains
more than one man-machine relationship. Hence, the focus in
this research is not on total industries or even on production
systems. The workers in each of the three samples had fellow
workers in their plants with quite dissimilar relationships to
technology.
Operationalization of technology in terms of nonmechanized,
mechanized, and automated man-machine relationships is crude
by design. The primary objective of the research is to observe
any differences in levels of alienation among workers in each
man-machine relationship. For factory workers an additional man-
machine relationship, machine tending, was not included in
the research design. To simplify the data-gathering process,
automobile assemblers were chosen to represent the mechanized
stage of production technology.

Table 1.1
Predicted Relationships between the Phases in the Man-Machine Relationship, Division of Labor and Alienation from Work* and Office and Factory Jobs Sampled

Phases in the Man-Machine Relationship	Division of Labor	Levels of Worker Alienation	Jobs Sampled	
			Office	Factory
Nonmechanized Workers	Lower Differentiation	Lower	Clerks of various grades and secretaries	Maintenance craftsmen in an automobile assembly plant
Mechanized Workers	Higher Differentiation	Higher	a. EDP: Key-punch operators; various punched-card equipment operators; proof-encoding machine operators b. Non-EDP: Production typists; Addressograph and microfilm operators	Final assembly-line automobile workers
Automated Workers	Lower Differentiation	Lower	a. Computer operators b. Computer software personnel (programmers and systems analysts)	Oil refinery control room monitors

* This part of the table is adapted from Faunce, "Automation and the Division of Labor," p. 153.

tained using the framework developed in these introductory pages can be interpreted. First, it will tell us something about the relationship between the division of labor and alienation from work among office and factory workers. Second, its use provides some insight into the historical trend in alienation from work as technology in the workplace has evolved from nonmechanization to mechanization to automation in certain contemporary white- and blue-collar industries.

In an earlier study,[21] the writer applied the man-machine relationship framework to the factory scene. Since most of the literature in this area focuses on blue-collar workers, continuity is enhanced by dealing first with the impact of technology on factory workers (Chapter 3). In Chapter 4 stages of technological change in the office are outlined, followed by a discussion of the impacts of technology on clerical work. An analysis of the effects of mechanization and computers on clerical employees occupies Chapter 5. A final analysis compares levels of alienation among factory and office workers. Before beginning a report of the findings, Chapter 2 is given over to the definition and measurement of alienation and to a description of the samples drawn from some offices and factories.

---

21. Jon M. Shepard, *Man-Machine Relationships, Attitudes Toward Work and Meanings in the Work Role,* Unpublished Doctoral Dissertation, Michigan State University, 1968.

Marx's heritage to social critics has proved bountiful. To social scientists interested in the concept of alienation, his ideas must be considered a mixed blessing. The major question is the separation of ideology surrounding Marx's ideas on alienation in order to turn them to scientific usefulness. In recent years social scientists have shown increasing interest in alienation as an empirically measurable concept. Seeman's contribution was to distinguish several uses of the concept alienation from the mass of sociological literature and to state them in a more empirically useful form.[1] Some of the variants of alienation discussed by Seeman are adopted here.

VARIANTS OF ALIENATION

Powerlessness

Marx's concern with the appropriation of the means of production by the entrepreneurs is the source of the powerlessness dimension of alienation. In the change from guild handicraft production to manufacturing in large factories, freedom and control were wrested from workers. In the work situation, powerlessness occurs when the worker feels that he is an object dominated and controlled by other people or a technological system of production such that, as subject, he cannot alter his condition.[2] Powerlessness refers to the perceived

---

1. Melvin Seeman, "On the Meaning of Alienation," *American Sociological Review*, 24 (December 1959), pp. 783–791.
2. Robert Blauner, *Alienation and Freedom* (Chicago: University of Chicago Press, 1964), p. 32.

lack of freedom and control on the job. These items form
the Powerlessness scale.[3]
1. To what extent can you vary the steps involved in
doing your job?
2. To what extent can you move from your immediate
working area during work hours?
3. To what extent can you control how much work you
produce?
4. To what extent can you help decide on methods and
procedures used in your job?
5. To what extent do you have influence over the things
that happen to you at work?
6. To what extent can you do your work ahead and
take a short rest break during work hours?
7. To what extent are you free from close supervision
while doing your job?
8. To what extent can you increase or decrease the speed
at which you work?

Meaninglessness
The meaninglessness variant of alienation refers to the
inability to understand the events in which one is engaged. With respect to work, meaninglessness sets in
when individual roles are perceived as lacking integration into the total system of goals of an organization.[4]
When workers know only their own specialized tasks and
do not, in the course of their work, come to know the
tasks of their co-workers, the function of other departments or how their work contributes to the company
product(s), they feel a loss of purpose and function.
Meaninglessness is operationalized with items referring

---

3. A description of the construction of all alienation scales is
contained in Appendix A.
4. Blauner, *Alienation and Freedom*, pp. 2–3.

to the lack of perceived relationship of one's job to the jobs of others and to the larger organization:
1. To what extent do you know how your job fits into the total plant (operations of the company)?
2. To what extent do you know how your job fits in with the work of other departments in the plant (company)?
3. To what extent do you know how your work relates to the work of others that you work with?

Normlessness
Durkheim's concern with the breakdown of the moral order, a condition of anomie, is the classical source of the normlessness variant of alienation. Anomie exists when there is a lack of socially approved means to reach culturally prescribed goals. Seeman refers to normlessness as the expectation that the achievement of culturally prescribed goals requires illegitimate means. Items in the Normlessness Scale were designed to measure the perceived extent to which upward mobility in the company required illegitimate tactics as opposed to achievement on the basis of merit:
1. To what extent do you feel that people who get ahead in the plant (company) deserve it?
2. To what extent do you feel that it is pull and connection that gets a person ahead in the plant (company)?
3. To what extent is getting ahead in the plant (company) based on ability?

Instrumental Work Orientation
The Marxian tradition holds "self-alienation" to be the heart of alienation in modern society. Seeman defines self-estrangement as "the degree of dependence of the given behavior upon anticipated future rewards, that

is, upon rewards that lie outside the activity itself." [5]
Self-estrangement is said to exist when an activity is
viewed as an instrumental rather than a consummatory
activity. Examples of this are men who work merely for
money or students who endure their academic training
merely for the sake of a degree that will get them a
"good" job.

After defining self-estrangement, Seeman points out
that it is difficult to specify what the alienation is from:
"to speak of 'alienation from the self' is after all simply
a metaphor, in a way that 'alienation from popular cul-
ture,' for example, need not be." [6] Consequently, the
latter can be concretely specified while the former pre-
sents greater difficulties. A more descriptive conceptual
label for Seeman's definition of self-estrangement is that
of instrumental orientation. Instrumental work orientation is conceptualized as the degree to which work is
valued primarily as a means to nonwork ends rather
than valued for its intrinsic rewards. The substitution of
instrumental orientation for self-estrangement is sound
for two reasons. First, Seeman recognizes the difficulty
in measuring alienation from the "self." Second, it
avoids confusion of this dimension with another variant
of alienation not dealt with by Seeman, that is, self-
evaluative involvement. Four items comprise the Instrumental Work Orientation Scale:
1. Your job is something you have to do to earn a living;
most of your real interests are centered outside your
job (occupation).
2. Money is the most rewarding reason for working.
3. Working is a necessary evil to provide things your
family and you want.
4. You are living for the day when you can collect your

---

5. Seeman, "On the Meaning of Alienation," p. 790.
6. *Ibid.,* p. 789.

retirement and do the things that are important
to you.

Self-Evaluative Involvement

Self-evaluative involvement refers to the degree to which
a person tests his self-esteem in terms of the status
criteria of a particular social unit of which he is a member. Self-evaluative involvement in work is concerned
with the degree to which one evaluates oneself with
regard to the work role. The two items forming the
Self-Evaluative Involvement Scale were designed to
reflect whether work or nonwork activity is the most
important in self-evaluation:
1. Success in the things you do away from the job is
more important to your opinion of yourself than
success in your work (occupational) career.
2. To you, your work (occupation) is only a small part
of who you are.
    Persons who are characterized by low self-evaluative
involvement in work evaluate themselves primarily in
terms of extrawork status criteria. There is, however,
in this study no specification of what these values or
goals might be, except that they are related to nonwork
roles.

SAMPLES AND RESEARCH INSTRUMENTS

In order to discern the effects of job attributes on worker
attitudes in different kinds of technological environ-
ments, a quota method was used whereby only workers
performing tasks corresponding to the different stages
of technological development were selected. For office
work, samples were obtained from a large bank, a large
insurance company, and four small insurance companies. Two industries, oil refining and automobile
manufacturing in combination, provided workers in
the three man-machine relationships for factory work.

Table 2.1 contains the results of the sampling process in the home offices of the five insurance companies and the bank. This table shows, by company and by phases in the man-machine relationship, sample sizes and the percentage of the total possible respondents that each sample represents.

For electronic data-processing jobs (that is, programmers, systems analysts, key-punch operators, tabulating equipment operators, and computer operators), saturation sampling in each organization was attempted. This was feasible since electronic data-processing units are well defined and do not employ large numbers of people. The return rates for employees in jobs directly related to the computer system were mixed, ranging from 45 percent to 100 percent.

Sampling nonelectronic data-processing personnel presented a quite different problem since they constitute the bulk of the clerical work force. A decision was made to get from each company a sample of nonelectronic data-processing clerical employees representing a wide range of job grades.

In the case of insurance companies B, C, and E, personnel managers unsystematically selected employees to participate, attempting to include as many job grades as possible. There is no defined unit which these employees represent. All clerical personnel in a nonelectronic data-processing department in insurance company D were asked to fill out the questionnaire. Seventy percent of this unit returned completed forms. In these four small insurance companies the questionnaires, placed in stamped envelopes addressed to the Sloan School of Management at M.I.T., were given to employees to take home and mail when completed.

Insurance company A permitted clerical employees in

Table 2.1
White-Collar Samples by Company and Phases in the Man-Machine Relationship

	Insurance Companies										Bank		Total
	A		B		C		D		E				
	Sample Size	% of Unit Sampled	Sample Size	% of Unit Sampled	Sample Size	% of Unit Sampled	Sample Size	% of Unit Sampled	Sample Size	% of Unit Sampled	Sample Size	% of Unit Sampled	Total
Nonmechanized Clerical Employees													
Traditional Clerks[a]	641	76%	27	*	24	*	64	70%	44	●	215	90%	1015
Mechanized Clerical Employees													
EDP[b]	98	70%	17	55%	23	100%	9	45%	17	82%	116	80%	280
Non-EDP[c]	87	†	12	*	26	*	33	†	11	*	88	†	257
Automated Clerical Employees													
Computer Console Operators	49	64%	3	50%	13	87%	1	50%	4	57%	52	87%	122
Software Personnel[d]	90	73%	13	65%	16	94%	9	100%	15	50%	71	62%	214
Total	965		72		102		116		91		542		1888

[a] Clerks of various sorts and secretaries.
[b] Key-punch, other punched-card equipment operators, and proof-encoding machine operators.
[c] Production typists of all kinds, Addressograph and microfilm operators.
[d] Programmers and systems analysts.
* These workers were selected unsystematically by supervisors. No identifiable units exist.
† Separate percentages were not calculated for nonmechanized and non-EDP mechanized clerical employees. Rather, all those in non-EDP departments were combined. In insurance company A, for example, 641 (traditional clerks) was added to 87 (non-EDP machine operators) and divided by the total possible respondents from non-EDP departments. This yielded a return of 76%. This percentage appears only under nonmechanized clerical employees, but should be understood to include non-EDP employees holding machine-operating jobs.

four departments outside the electronic data-processing division to fill out the questionnaire while at work. One participating department was the stenographic pool, containing women who typed using dictating equipment. The other three departments were chosen because they represented varying degrees of interconnection with the computer system. Of the employees in these departments combined, 76 percent returned completed questionnaires.

In the bank, five departments of a large nonelectronic data-processing division were sampled. One of these departments contained employees whose jobs were very much tied to the computer system. The other four departments were much less affected by computerization. Questionnaires were completed in groups on company time. Ninety percent of the employees in these five departments returned answered questionnaires.

Samples: Factory Workers

The respondent selection process in the oil refinery, hereafter referred to as Circle Oil, involved an attempted saturation sample of operators in the plant. This industrial complex included two plants. Operations in the number one plant were manned by 32 monitors. Of these, 20 (63 percent) consented to interviews. Plant number two was larger, requiring 77 operators. Seventy-two (94 percent) were interviewed. This yielded a total of 92 workers in the automated production category.

According to the seniority list dated December 31, 1966, the UAW local had an approximate membership of 12,000. Total number of workers on the "assembly power controlled line" was 1,252. Nearly half of this number did not conform to the man-machine relationship criterion; that is, they performed jobs not directly on the final assembly line. The universe of final assembly-line workers in this plant was 690. Excluded from this number were those with less than a year's seniority. A table of random numbers was used to select a sample of 150 workers. Of this original sample 30 were legitimately eliminated, leaving 120 to be interviewed. Those eliminated were either in military service, female, trainees, retired, or no longer working at the auto plant. The final sample ($N = 120$) is 17 percent[7] of the plant population of final assemblers. Of these 120, 96 (80 percent) were actually interviewed.

Including employees in training, maintenance and engineering journeymen totaled 1,907. Journeymen in maintenance,[8] excluding apprentices, formed the universe for the plant ($N = 573$). By a table of random numbers a sample of 150 journeymen was selected. Seven of the 150 were eliminated since they were either retired, quit, deceased, or were still apprentices. The actual potential sample ($N = 143$) constitutes a 25 percent sample of the plant population of maintenance craftsmen. Eighty-two percent of the 143 maintenance craftsmen ($N = 117$) consented to interviews.

The data used to construct alienation indexes for blue-collar workers were obtained from a series of closed-response statements contained in an interview schedule requiring just over an hour to complete. Administration of the instrument to Circle Oil employees took place on the job. The UAW local union provided names and addresses of persons in the samples selected. Interviews were conducted in consenting workers' homes.

---

7. This percentage and the analogous one for maintenance craftsmen are approximate. They are based on totals that do not take into account people who should have been dropped from or added to the union list at the time the samples were selected.
8. Skilled trades included pipefitters, welders, machine repairmen, electricians, millwrights, carpenters, tinsmiths, and pneumatic tool repairmen.

Due to the number of companies involved and the size of the sample, it was decided to use a questionnaire based on the original interview schedule among white-collar employees. Among the four small insurance companies, the questionnaires were completed by employees while off the job and returned in stamped envelopes, preaddressed to the Sloan School of Management at M.I.T. In the large insurance company the data-collection procedure was a mixture of this method and employees completing the questionnaire in groups while at work. The bank permitted all employees included in the study to fill out the form in groups on company time.

Marx's ideas on "alienated labor" were the product of a man witnessing the institution-shattering economic and technological forces unleashed by the industrial revolution. The difficulty lies not so much in Marx's observations as in the error of overgeneralization committed by Marx and his intellectual heirs. The truth in the criticisms advanced by Marx and some other nineteenth- and twentieth-century thinkers did not warrant the application of a perspective based on the impact of industrialization in its incipient stage to industrial society as a whole.[1]

To this overgeneralization may be added a second. Dividing society into workers and owners necessarily sharpens the differences between the two classes, while at the same time blurring distinctions within either class. Similarly, the assumption of the existence of a homogeneous category, called the industrial worker, is inaccurate; variations in blue-collar work exist. Industrialization did not eliminate all craftlike jobs, and we have not seen the final stage of development in industrial production technology.

In Chapter 1, our study showed that work attitudes were negatively related to the degree of differentiation in the division of labor. Three such degrees of differentiation were distinguished in the historical development of manufacturing technology. Functional specialization tends to be low in craft production systems, reaches a peak in mechanized production systems, and is reduced under automated technology. Three types of workers—craftsmen, machine operators, and ma-

---

1. Reinhard Bendix, *Work and Authority in Industry* (New York: Harper & Row, Publishers, 1963), p. viii.

chine monitors—represent crucial relationships to technology in nonmechanized, mechanized, and automated types of production technology. Samples of maintenance craftsmen from an automobile manufacturing factory, assembly-line workers in the same automobile factory, and control-room monitors in an oil refinery were selected to represent these three man-machine relationships. On the basis of Blauner's findings, the expectation is that assemblers will exhibit the highest levels of alienation from work, while craftsmen and monitors will be considerably less alienated. Demonstration that this is indeed the case among the present samples of factory workers is the task of this chapter.

MAN-MACHINE RELATIONSHIPS AND WORKER ALIENATION

Powerlessness

A strong curvilinear relationship appears between the phases in the man-machine relationship and the degree of perceived powerlessness on the job (Table 3.1). It is clear from the percentages that few craftsmen (19 percent) experience lack of freedom and control in their

Table 3.1
Perceived Powerlessness in Work by Phases in the Man-Machine Relationship

Perceived Powerlessness in Work	Phases in the Man-Machine Relationship		
	Craft ($N = 113$)	Mechanized ($N = 93$)	Automated ($N = 85$)
Above Median	19%	94%	42%
Below Median	81	6	58
Total	100	100	100

$X^2 = 114.67$, $df = 2$, $P < .001$, $\overline{C} = .77$

24 Industrial Workers

work. At the other extreme, 94 percent of the assemblers feel a sense of powerlessness. For monitors, less than half (42 percent) are on the high end of the Powerlessness Scale. A sense of powerlessness at work is at a low point among craftsmen, extends to a high peak among assemblers, and among monitors descends to a point higher than craftsmen (a difference of 23 percent) but lower than final assembly-line workers (a difference of 52 percent).

The absence of freedom and control is related to the phases in the man-machine relationship and the division of labor, in that extreme functional specialization normally occurs under a mechanized production system characterized by mechanical pacing of work and predetermination in the use of tools and techniques. Rationalization precludes worker decisions regarding methods and procedures used in a job and does not allow for much variation in the manner of completing one's task(s). Who does what and how is very meticulously engineered. It is difficult to vary the way in which one does a job when the number of operations is limited to one or, at best, a few.

Mechanical control of the work pace, characteristic of the assembly-line mode of production, is a prominent source of dislike among automobile workers because it has several important negative consequences. Mechanical pacing results in the relative absence of control over the dispensation of time on the part of the worker. A limited number of operations must be performed within a time period geared to the speed of the conveyors. When a finished automobile rolls off the line at the speed of one per minute, little control over the speed at which one works is permitted. Working up the line to get ahead of the pace is possible for some assembly-line workers. However, it is in the logic of the assembly-line mode of production that the speed of the line be closely geared to the time required for a set of operations.

The statement about wishing the line would break down made by one of the workers in the Walker and Guest study reflects the feeling among assembly-line workers that what they do on the job depends on the technology. If the line breaks down, freedom and control are temporarily theirs.

Most jobs on the line are done within a very limited spatial span and at a rapid clip. Consequently, lack of movement from the immediate working area has real meaning. Breaks can be taken only when a relief man is there to take over. This restriction of physical movement along with the spatial distribution of assemblers and the noise and speed of the line curtail social interaction. The result is limited control over the social environment. Control over how much work an assembler does is preempted because quantity of production depends on the pace at which the conveyor is set to move.

Continuous-process technology returns some freedom and control to industrial workers in the form of control over work pace, some latitude in the selection of work procedures, and movement from the immediate work area. At set intervals during the shift, each operator in the oil refinery checks a panel of indicators and records these readings. At one time the operator will check the instrument panel in the control room. After a designated period he will leave the control room to monitor the indicators on the production unit outside for which he is responsible. At Circle Oil, operators made readings every two hours in the control room, and once every half hour or hour they checked the production unit outside the control room. From this brief description it is evident that monitors are subject to little mechanical pacing. They can perform their tasks at a speed suited to their nature or temporary mood. Freedom and control with regard to methods and procedures is permitted through operator discretion in making and recording readings. Dials and gauges can be read with considerable variation in time. An operator, for example, may take his readings early in order to eat at a time more attuned to his appetite, or he may choose to eat first and delay a scheduled reading. And tasks can be accomplished with variation in the sequence in which they are done.

Supervision is normally quite loose, and orders are given only during periods of emergency. The number one operator is technically the unit supervisor, but operators are oriented normally toward the technology for directives. Of course, errors are easily traced to their source, and the danger and costliness of mistakes promote frequent checking of that section of the instrument panel for which each operator is responsible.

Operators cannot leave the plant during their shift. Control rooms are equipped with ovens and refrigerators for meals and snacks. Physical movement, however, is not as limited as first impression indicates. Operators can leave the control room at any time to smoke (smoking in the control room is prohibited due to the high inflammability of the products) or otherwise take a break. Only the number one operator is severely restricted to the control room, and he can leave when the number two operator is in the unit. Additional freedom of movement is interjected as part of the operator's job: as already mentioned, at frequent intervals the operator leaves the control room to check the production unit(s) outside for which he is responsible.

Except during emergencies operators are at liberty to dispense time in a variety of ways. Upon entering a control room one can regularly expect to see at least two or three operators talking together. Since they are free during intervals between readings, they can spend time talking, reading, smoking, or eating. In the interview one question asked operators if they enjoyed their work more than their leisure time. To get clarification, one refinery operator queried, "Do you mean leisure time on the job or off the job?" The feeling among monitors that they exercise a great deal of influence over what they do while at work is apparent.

In traditional craft jobs the division of labor is based on craft specialization which entails making the total product or contributing to large segments of the product. Fashioning shoes by hand prior to mechanization is one of many examples of traditional craft work. Maintenance craftsmen in industrial organizations are specialized along craft lines. In the auto plant studied, skilled maintenance trades included pipe fitters, welders, machine repairmen, electricians, millwrights, carpenters, tinsmiths, and pneumatic tool repairmen. The maintenance journeymen are certified by the union normally after serving a three- or four-year apprenticeship. Consequently, they are highly skilled workers as measured by their degree of manual dexterity, exercise of judgment, and the length of time required to learn their trade.

Maintenance craftsmen are exposed to a variety of work situations requiring application of the manual dexterity, knowledge, and skills they have acquired. It is within their power to control the quantity of work they do. They are free to choose the appropriate tools, materials, and work methods from a backlog of experience. Such decisions are made often to match the frequently changing job assignments. Maintenance craftsmen are generally issued an assignment or perhaps a list of jobs at the day's beginning. From that point they enjoy a high degree of freedom from direct supervision and have wide latitude in the dispensation of their work time. Their work implements are manually controlled tools that permit them to determine their work pace and to regulate the degree of pressure to suit their personal needs except under emergency conditions.

Meaninglessness

It is apparent from Table 3.2 that the phases in the man-machine relationship are related in the predicted curvilinear direction to perceived meaninglessness in work at a statistically reliable level. Almost the same percentage of craftsmen and monitors are high on the Meaninglessness Scale. Forty-six percent of the craftsmen and 45 percent of the monitors are above the median on the Meaninglessness Scale. Among assemblers, nearly three-fourths exhibit a lack of knowledge of the relationship of their jobs to the jobs of others and to the larger organization.

The effects of the division of labor are most clearly seen in the experience of meaninglessness. Several factors contribute to the fact that maintenance craftsmen know a great deal about the operation of the larger plant and consequently have considerable perception of how their work is related to the work of others and to

Table 3.2
Perceived Meaninglessness in Work by Phases in the Man-Machine Relationship

Perceived Meaninglessness in Work	Phases in the Man-Machine Relationship		
	Craft ($N = 113$)	Mechanized ($N = 93$)	Automated ($N = 85$)
Above Median	46%	73%	45%
Below Median	54	27	55
Total	100	100	100

$X^2 = 19.55$, $df = 2$, $P < .001$, $\overline{C} = .36$

the larger organization. First, they exercise their skills in the performance of jobs that require a number of operations, and they are oriented toward the completion of a total job. Second, maintenance craftsmen are called upon to work in many areas of the plant and may even have a number of separate jobs on any given day. Consequently, their coverage of the plant is considerable. Third, a particular job often demands men from several crafts, whether for technical or craft boundary maintenance reasons. Observation of men from other crafts at work increases the knowledge of interconnections among jobs.

Blauner reiterated the argument that when mechanization evolved in the factory system, the division of labor became increasingly subdivided, thus leaving the factory worker with a job largely devoid of purpose and function. Performing one or a few small operations out of the entire production process robs machine operators, in this case assembly-line workers, of a sense of the connection of their jobs to the jobs of others or to the purposes of the larger organization. They know only their own limited tasks and need not know the tasks of other workers, jobs performed in other departments, or how their work relates to the operations of the larger organization.

Several factors related to the division of labor account for the findings that continuous-process operators feel less of a sense of meaninglessness than do the assembly-line workers. In the first place, as Blauner points out, "the most characteristic feature of automation is its transfer of focus from an individual job to the process of production. The perspective of the worker is shifted from his own individual tasks to a broader series of operations that includes the work of other employees." [2]

2. Robert Blauner, *Alienation and Freedom* (Chicago: University of Chicago Press, 1964), pp. 172–173.

The production processes under automated technology are integrated and continuous. In oil refining, for example, crude oil derivatives are transported from one processing unit to another by an overhead and underground complex of pipes and reactors. Products, from their introduction into the system as crude oil until pumps release them into transport vehicles, are not touched by human hands. A reduction in the division of labor with continuous-process technology can be attributed to the reduction, by integration and continuous flow, of the number of separate operations and a linking together of the responsibilities of the few workers manning a control room. The fulfillment of each man's responsibility is a unique contribution to the smooth functioning of the total system. While an assembler can attach a headlight with little thought to the total product, operators in a continuous-process production system must refer to the total production system. A malfunction in one operator's area of responsibility can ruin an entire batch of the product.

A second factor promoting worker attention to the larger production system in a continuous-process operating job is the physical danger involved in the processing of volatile products. The expense of spoilage, which may run into astronomical proportions rather quickly, is a third factor.

A fourth factor is that continuous-process technology reduces the number of separate job classifications. As observed earlier, this reduction is due to the integration into a continuous flow of many discrete tasks formerly performed by individual workers. Large manufacturing plants are predicated on a rather extensive and intensive division of labor. While craftsmen, for example, may not have highly specialized jobs themselves, they are working within a production system comprised of an almost infinitely large number of separate job classi-

fications. No data were collected on the number of
separate job classifications in the automobile factory
included in this study. But in the automobile plant
studied by Chinoy there were over 150 different "non-
interchangeable occupational groups." On the average
each occupational group was comprised of four or five
job classifications. Some occupational groups had as
many as twenty to thirty separate job classifications.[3]
In sharp contrast, the job classifications in the two Circle
Oil plants were limited to maintenance craftsmen,
control-room operators, pumpers, boiler operators, tank
car cleaners, truck loaders, garage mechanics, janitors,
and laborers.

A fifth factor contributing to the low level of meaninglessness among monitors lies in the job classification
system in control rooms at Circle Oil. In the control
rooms operating positions are numbered, the number
of levels varying with the size of the control room. An
operator is assigned to the highest numbered position
when he begins work in a control room. Any advancement is to the next operator classification level. This
means that by the time an operator works his way up
to become the number one operator, he has held all
those operating jobs below. Knowledge of operating
jobs held in the past and anticipation of movement
to the next level(s) promote understanding of the interconnections among various operating functions. Given
these characteristics, it is easy to understand why meaninglessness is less likely to develop among monitors in

---

3. Ely Chinoy, *Automobile Workers and the American Dream*
(Garden City, New York: Doubleday & Company, Inc., 1955), p.
39. Because the same jobs in different plant divisions were not
classified into the same occupational group, it is impossible to
say how many distinct job classifications existed in this plant.
But it is obvious that on a plant-wide basis the division of labor
was quite elaborate.

a continuous-process production system than among workers in mechanized jobs.

Normlessness

Table 3.3 attests to a curvilinear relationship between the phases in the man-machine relationship and the degree of perceived normlessness in work. Smaller percentage differences among the three types of workers indicate that this relationship is not as strong as in the first two hypotheses tested. Nevertheless, the relationship is significant at the .001 level, and the degree of association ($\overline{C} = .32$) is reasonable. A greater percentage difference obtains between monitors and assemblers high on the Normlessness Scale (33 percent compared to 61 percent) than for either of the other comparisons. Slightly less than half (48 percent) of the craftsmen are high on the Normlessness Scale, while 61 percent of the assemblers are similarly classified. Normlessness appears to be more prevalent among the automobile workers regardless of their jobs (craftsmen, 48 percent; assemblers, 61 percent) as compared to the oil refinery monitors (33 percent).

Normlessness, or the perceived lack of promotion

Table 3.3
Perceived Normlessness in Work by Phases in the Man-Machine Relationship

Perceived Normlessness in Work	Phases in the Man-Machine Relationship		
	Craft ($N = 113$)	Mechanized ($N = 93$)	Automated ($N = 85$)
Above Median	48%	61%	33%
Below Median	52	39	67
Total	100	100	100

$X^2 = 14.31$, $df = 2$, $P < .001$, $\overline{C} = .32$

through legitimate means, is associated with the division of labor because extreme functional specialization creates a large number of occupational specialties among which there are few differentiations in either skill level or wages. It is alleged that bureaucratic organizations promote on the basis of merit. However, Chinoy found among automobile assembly-line workers

that persistent effort, a good performance record, and faithful adherence to company rules, all sanctioned by tradition and encouraged by management as representing evidence of merit and ability, were not in themselves enough to gain promotion; and that whatever a man's other qualifications, he also needed pull or connections in order to become a foreman.[4]

This attitude most likely reflects frustration with perceived inability to rise occupationally. Factors contributing to the feeling of few mobility opportunities among assemblers are the compressed wage scale and the lack of a hierarchical arrangement of job classifications to which workers can aspire. Placing blame upon the system rather than upon themselves, these workers are led to comments such as, "It's one-third ability and two-thirds pull."

Because of the operator hierarchy existing in the oil refinery control rooms, workers at Circle Oil expect that they will be promoted to the next level above them. And those who have advanced in the hierarchy can see that there are job grades below them. The attitude that people are promoted on the basis of pull and connection is less likely to develop where an occupational hierarchy such as this exists.

Normlessness among craftsmen is expected to be lower than among assemblers, as Chinoy's comment indicates: Pull and connections were widely looked upon as the major supplements to or alternatives for merit and ability as

4. *Ibid.,* p. 53.

prerequisites for foremanship, although, it should be noted, this view seemed to be less prevalent among skilled workers whose technical competence, initiative, and leadership could be more readily appraised.[5]
Moreover, normlessness is curtailed among craftsmen who, by nature of having gone through an apprenticeship program to reach their status, have a sense of having achieved upward occupational mobility.

SELF-EVALUATIVE INVOLVEMENT IN WORK AND INSTRUMENTAL WORK ORIENTATION

In order to relate the phases in the man-machine relationship to self-evaluative involvement in work and instrumental work orientation, it is useful to present some ideas derived from social psychological theory.[6] Some theorists[7] postulate that a person's evaluation of himself relative to social roles is a selective rather than a random process. Activities that permit a man to see himself in a favorable light are more likely to be used as referents by which he judges the kind of person he thinks he is. A person tends to evaluate himself in terms of social situations that confirm his worth. Social situations that are not so rewarding are devalued.

As Faunce points out, every social unit, whether it is a family or a total society, has a status structure, that is, "a hierarchy of persons based upon the extent to which they are accorded social honor." [8] Assignment of social honor or status recognition rests on achievement in terms of relevant status criteria. The number of status

---

5. *Ibid.*, p. 54.
6. An elaboration of these ideas may be found in William A. Faunce, *Problems of an Industrial Society* (New York: McGraw-Hill Book Company, 1968), pp. 90–97.
7. Hans L. Zetterberg, "Complaint Actions," *Acta Sociologia,* 2 (1957), pp. 179–201, and Gardner Murphy, *Personality* (New York: Harper and Brothers, Publishers, 1947).
8. Faunce, *The Problems of an Industrial Society,* p. 93.

criteria may range from one, as in the case of speed in track, to many, like a married male who is expected among other things to be a good husband, father, and provider. High placement in a status structure means that one has been evaluated favorably by others on important status criteria and has achieved marked status recognition. Since status recognition rests on the evaluation of others in the status structure, it constitutes social support for positive self-evaluation. To the extent that a person can attain status recognition, he presumably can maintain or enhance favorable self-evaluation. Assuming that low self-esteem is something to be avoided, the proposition follows that the lack of status recognition, and consequently the absence of social support for positive self-evaluation, will tend to produce a withdrawal of self-esteem testing from that status structure.[9]

There is a corollary to this proposition. The failure to achieve status recognition leads to the abandonment of commitment to participation in the status structure. A man participates in an activity, all the while conserving himself for endeavors outside the activity which he considers much more important. Such a response constitutes an instrumental orientation. That is, he remains a participant in an activity only for what it permits him to do while not in that activity. People who work only for the uses to which their paychecks can be put fall into this category.[10]

---

9. This conception of alienation has been stated by Faunce, *Ibid.*, p. 94.
10. Social psychological withdrawal, of course, is not the only adaptation to the perceived lack of status recognition. An extreme reaction would be to withdraw physically from the situation, as might be the case for some high school "dropouts" who feel they cannot compete. Remaining in the situation but shifting energies to other aspects of the status structure is another re-

These ideas permit the proposition that failure to achieve status recognition within a status structure promotes alienation from that status structure. The present study takes alienation from work as one special case of the broader theoretical framework. In the status structure of the workplace, freedom and control, knowledge of interrelationships among jobs, and the opportunity to advance on the basis of merit are viewed as status criteria.[11] Perceived high ranking on the dimensions of freedom control, meaning, and the possibility of mobility based on ability provide status recognition at work. Conversely, experience of powerlessness, meaninglessness, and normlessness in work each contribute to alienation from work.

Work situations that promote feelings of powerlessness, meaninglessness, and normlessness impede the achievement of status recognition in the work status structure. Such a lack of status recognition contributes

---

sponse. For example, boys who do not feel adequate in sporting competition or who do not feel attractive to girls may turn their energies away from the "popular" status structure in school and concentrate on achievement in studies. Faunce mentions two other possible responses. One is to exert increased effort to achieve in the status structure with the belief that the relative lack of status recognition is temporary. Another path is to judge oneself to be a failure. Given the assumption of the desire to maximize self-evaluation, it could be predicted that those who do not succeed after trying harder will discontinue self-esteem testing in that activity. And a feeling of failure over time will most likely lead to a withdrawal of self-esteem testing from that activity. It is true that some people never stop trying, some delude themselves, and there are those who consider themselves failures as a continual judgment. A point Faunce makes is that social psychological withdrawal is a common reaction to low status as well as a more stable response than other possible ones.

11. There are perhaps more important status criteria such as skill and income. However, these status criteria lie outside the alienation framework.

Table 3.4
Self-Evaluative Involvement in the Work Role by Phases in the
Man-Machine Relationship

Self-Evaluative Involvement in Work	Phases in the Man-Machine Relationship		
	Craft ($N = 117$)	Mechanized ($N = 96$)	Automated ($N = 92$)
Above Median	48%	38%	70%
Below Median	52	62	30
Total	100	100	100

$X^2 = 19.09$, $df = 2$, $P < .001$, $\overline{C} = .35$

to alienation from work. At this point an inference is
necessary. Curvilinear relationships were found between the phases in the man-machine relationships and
powerlessness, meaninglessness, and normlessness. It
follows that self-evaluative involvement in work and
instrumental work orientation should be related to the
phases in the man-machine relationship in a similar
pattern.[12]

The hypothesized curvilinear relationship between the
phases in the man-machine relationship and self-evaluative involvement in work is supported at the .001 level
of significance (Table 3.4). Forty-eight percent of the
craftsmen are high in terms of the extent to which they
used the work role for evaluating themselves. This is
the case for 38 percent of the assemblers. A larger percentage of monitors is above the median on the Self-

12. An obvious alternative is to test directly the relationships
between powerlessness, meaninglessness and normlessness, and
self-evaluative involvement and instrumental work orientation.
This approach is left for development elsewhere. Of central concern now are the relationships between the phases in the man-
machine relationships and alienation from work.

Evaluative Involvement scale (70 percent) than either craftsmen or assemblers.

Table 3.5 shows the results of the cross-tabulation between the phases in the man-machine relationship and the Instrumental Work Orientation scale. The feeling that their jobs are merely a means to ends outside of work is the most prominent among automobile assemblers. Sixty-nine percent of these workers are above the median on the Instrumental Work Orientation scale. A sharp contrast is found among control-room operators in the oil refinery. Only 29 percent fail to find their work intrinsically meaningful. Of the maintenance craftsmen in the automobile factory, one-half are instrumentally oriented. It is clear that the relegation of work to the status of a means for the pursuance of nonwork activities is lower among craftsmen, rises to a peak among assemblers, and dips to a markedly lower level among monitors in a continuous-process production system.

SUMMARY

The impact of technology on alienation from work among factory workers was examined through com-

Table 3.5
Instrumental Work Orientation by Phases in the Man-Machine Relationship

Instrumental Work Orientation	Phases in the Man-Machine Relationship		
	Craft ($N = 113$)	Mechanized ($N = 93$)	Automated ($N = 85$)
Above Median	50%	69%	29%
Below Median	50	31	71
Total	100	100	100

$X^2 = 27.59$, $df = 2$, $P < .001$, $\overline{C} = .46$

parisons of samples representing craft, mechanized, and automated man-machine relationships. Curvilinear associations were found between the phases in the man-machine relationship and each of five alienation scales (Powerlessness, Meaninglessness, Normlessness, Self-Evaluative Involvement, and Instrumental Work Orientation). With one exception, alienation was lower among craftsmen, reached a peak among assemblers, and declined again among monitors to a level below that of either assemblers or craftsmen. The exception had to do with the powerlessness dimension of alienation. A curvilinear relationship similar to the others appeared, but monitors were somewhat more powerless with regard to work than craftsmen. Some implications of these findings will be advanced in Chapter 7, along with a discussion of the effects of technology on alienation from work among clerical employees.

4 The Changing Nature of Office Work

In Chapter 3 findings were presented that substantiate the existence of variations in alienation from work among blue-collar workers who labor under distinctively different relationships to technology. Evidence from the research of others is presented in this chapter which suggests that the application of different types of technology to information processing has created man-machine relationships in the office similar to those in the factory. Do similar relationships to technology in the office and factory produce similar patterns in alienation from work? This question will be put to empirical test in Chapter 5. Prior to this analysis several stages of technological development will be delineated for the office. Then the impact of technological change on the nature of clerical work is examined, relating computerization to the phases in the man-machine relationship.

STAGES OF TECHNOLOGICAL CHANGE IN THE OFFICE
A detailed description of the nature of business machines from primitive typewriters to computers is not the intention here. What follows is an adumbration of the major stages in the application of machines to paperwork. It is quite clear that these stages are not distinct in the sense that one type of technology totally replaced another. In fact, modern computerized offices contain machines of the sort characteristic of each previous stage of mechanization.

Craft Stage
Technological changes in the office follow roughly the pattern described for the factory. Several stages of tech-

nological change in the office may be distinguished.[1]
Prior to mechanization office work was comparable to
the craft period in blue-collar industries. Like the blue-
collar sector, the pure craft period in office work pre-
ceded mechanization when, for example, a company
bookkeeper needed only a pen, ledger, and his arithmetical ability. In highly computerized offices today
there are many clerical workers, such as secretaries and
clerks of various kinds, who perform tasks without the
direct use of any mechanical means. Many of these
clerical employees holding nonmechanized jobs are
affected indirectly by a computer system to the extent
that their work is related to input or output. Despite
this, they belong in the craft or nonmechanized man-
machine relationship, since they perform a number of
tasks in a fashion that is not directly determined
technologically.

Early Mechanization
In order to handle the expanding amount of information that had to be processed, offices were forced to
introduce mechanization. Embryonic office mechanization appeared in the latter part of the nineteenth
century. Early office technology such as typewriters,
adding machines, and dictating machines were designed
to perform single functions. In general, these technological developments did not alter the tradition of manual
processing of information. This stage of mechanization

1. The description of the stages of mechanization in the office
draws heavily from a series of articles in the *International Labor
Review*. See "Effects of Mechanisation and Automation in Offices:
I," *International Labor Review,* 81 (February 1960), pp. 154–173;
"Effects of Mechanisation and Automation in Offices: II," *International Labor Review,* 81 (March 1960), pp. 255–273; Except
for direct quotes, no specific citations with reference to these
articles are made.

in the office is best characterized by clerical employees utilizing rather simple machines as adjuncts to the several functions they perform. Skills are not built into the machines, but rather abilities possessed by employees are brought to bear on the equipment in the course of performing varied work tasks. This is quite clear in the case of simple machines such as typewriters and adding machines:

. . . it is deceptive to speak of displacement of skills during the early days of office mechanization. What these machines really replaced was a great deal of laborious manual effort in copying and checking data and routine arithmetical calculations; the skills required in this work had been mainly acquired through practice, and a good general education, a knowledge of office routines, and some understanding of the business continued to be the desirable qualifications of the clerical worker, whether his work was done by manual or mechanical means.[2]

The application of these technological innovations brought about no significant skill and job content changes in office work.

Multifunction business machines appeared after the First World War, ushering in further developments in office mechanization prior to punched-card and electronic data-processing technology. More marked infringement on manual clerical skills came about with the introduction of technological devices that could perform a number of functions. Training in accounting, for example, was no longer necessary for bookkeeping clerks as the latter became operators of machines.

So far, the description of early mechanization in the office deals only with the intrinsic nature of the technology. Nothing has been said about the various ways in which a particular level of technology may be used in

2. "Effects of Mechanisation and Automation in Offices: II," p. 255.

performing clerical tasks. These machines may be util-
ized today as they were initially, as an aid to the clerk
in the performance of a number of tasks. Another alternative, resulting in increased job specialization, is the
concentration of machines on a functional basis. The
secretarial pool, where female clerks type on a full-time
basis, is an excellent example of the employment of a
low-level technological device to create a number of
specialized, machine-operating jobs.

In the sampling procedure of the present study, a
distinction is made between clerks who use simple
machines as adjuncts to their work and those who are
full-time machine operators as a result of machine
arrangement. The work attitudes of the latter are expected to be more in line with special-purpose machine
operators in punched-card data-processing systems, the
next stage of office mechanization, than with the attitudes
of office employees for which simple machines are
merely aids to their larger jobs.

Punched-Card Data Processing

Just as typewriters and other office machines had earlier
become part of the office scene, electromechanical or
punched-card data processing systems have been adopted
in order to cope with the meteoric expansion of data
to be handled in business organizations. Punched-card
data-processing systems were first used by the federal
government as early as 1890. However, this form of
technology did not gain significant impetus in the office
until after 1945.

The punched-card system of data processing involves
the recording and storing of data by means of perforated
cards. Punched data cards are passed through sorting
machines operating on the basis of electrical impulses.
Machines tabulate and print results from these cards.
Revolutionary effects on the nature of some types of

office work resulted from the application of punched-card technology to clerical functions. Many machine operators had to be recruited to man tabulating, sorting, key-punching, interpreting, collating, and reproducing machines. The new class of office worker, the semiskilled machine operator, was expanded. Many earlier machines were auxiliary to clerical functions; these new machines consumed many of the tasks formerly performed manually. Business experience or educational background as requisites for qualifications were replaced by machine-operating skills.

Electronic Data Processing

The most recent technological innovation is the application of electronic computers to data processing. The uniqueness of computer technology lies in its speed, accuracy, storage capacity, and ability to perform for long, uninterrupted periods of time. With regard to speed, as early as 1958 a large-scale computer in a government installation could perform computations in about half an hour which would require a year's time for one person operating a desk calculator.[3] Another source reports that a computer is "capable of performing . . . 300,000 additions, or 2,400 multiplications of 10 digits by 10 digits in one minute." [4] In the reception room of a highly computerized bank's data-processing center is a display showing on one side a large ledger book used in the nineteenth century and on the other a few pages of computer output. This quote appears in the display: "Today, high speed computers make it

---

3. U.S. Department of Labor, Bureau of Labor Statistics Bulletin Number 1241, *Automation and Employment Opportunites for Office Workers* (Washington, D.C.: U.S. Government Printing Office, 1958), p. 2.
4. "Effects of Mechanisation and Automation in Offices: I," p. 159.

possible to record the daily average of 275,000 trans-
actions made by the 135,000 checking account customers
of the [Bank]. . . . Incidentally, it would take the
computer ¾ second to print out everything you see on
the two pages of the [Bank] ledger book." Outside of
mechanical malfunction or a programming error, the
accuracy of the computer is quite high. There have been
attempts to check accuracy of the computer, but in
one reported case this procedure was abandoned because
all of the mistakes found were committed by humans
during the checking process.[5]

Another unique feature of computers is their memory
or storage capacity. Earlier types of office equipment
such as accounting, bookkeeping, and tabulating machines operated on the internal storage principle, but
only for the short length of time while the operations
were being performed. The capacity of the computer
is infinitely larger and constantly being extended so
that information can be internally stored for any desired
length of time. One company included in the present
study first installed a small computer with a capacity
of 4,000 characters, later added a medium-sized computer
capable of storing 50,000 characters, and now has a
larger computer with a capacity of 256,000 characters.
Another of the companies has several computers, two
of which have a capacity of 512,000 characters each.
Furthermore, the development of disc drives and data
cell drives runs the character storage capacity into the
hundreds of millions.

A most important feature of this technology in terms
of the nature of computer operating jobs is the facility
for long, uninterrupted periods of functioning with a
minimum of human intervention. In addition to storing

5. E. R. F. W. Crossman, *Automation and Skill* (London: Her
Majesty's Stationery Office, 1960), p. 35.

data for future processing and carrying over partial results in a series of operations, the computer also stores programmed instructions. This facility for holding in memory a series of instructions for operations on incoming data is a radical departure from office technology in earlier stages of mechanization. Because computers can operate for long periods of time on the basis of internally contained instructions, the console operator's job involves monitoring as well as operating the computer.

TECHNOLOGY AND THE CHANGING NATURE OF CLERICAL WORK

For the most part, research has not focused on the impact of technology on the nature of clerical work, except as the latter has been affected by computerization. Despite the appearance of mechanization in the office via punched-card data processing and earlier forms of technological devices, most discussions and studies of technologically induced alterations in office work are from the viewpoint of the effects of electronic data processing. Reliance on literature with this focus is especially appropriate since each of the six offices included in this investigation has installed computers. It should be kept in mind that the man-machine relationship associated with punched-card data processing is the same whether or not the office has computers.[6]

Research permits the association of different degrees of functional specialization with nonmechanized, mechanized, and automated man-machine relationships in the office. The effort to support empirically the relationships between the stages of mechanization in the office

---

6. Some modifications may occur if technology such as the optical scanner begins to phase out parts of the punched-card step of data preparation for computer processing.

and variations in the degree of functional specialization rests partly on the inference that downgrading is usually accompanied by a diminution in job size and responsibility, and upgrading usually entails job enlargement and increased responsibility.

Research suggests that as a result of computerization the occupational structure in the office is generally upgraded.[7] From the study of five insurance companies of various sizes, Delehanty[8] found that punched-card and computer data-processing technology were associated with a reduction in company need for lower-level clerical workers and an increased demand for higher-level clerical employees. The Bureau of Labor Statistics conducted a study of 20 offices that had just installed large-scale electronic computers. Of those employees who were still with their companies at the end of this 18-month conversion study, just over two-thirds remained at the same grade level as before the introduction of computers, almost a third were in positions of a higher grade level, and only slightly over one percent had experienced downgrading.[9] Rico's[10] findings indicate that computer technology eliminates the most routine jobs (for example, filing and posting clerk's jobs) and increases the number of higher-level clerical

---

7. This point has to be qualified, since downgrading has also been found after conversion to electronic data processing. And all routine jobs will not be eliminated by computer technology.
8. George E. Delehanty, "Office Automation and Occupation Structure: A Case Study of Five Insurance Companies," *Industrial Management Review,* 7 (Spring 1966), p. 108.
9. U.S. Department of Labor, Bureau of Labor Statistics, *Adjustments to the Introduction of Office Automation,* Bulletin No. 1276 (Washington, D.C.: U.S. Government Printing Office, 1960), p. 33.
10. Leonard Rico, "The Staffing Process and the Computer," *Management of Personnel Quarterly,* 1 (Autumn–Winter 1962), p. 33.

positions. A study of an insurance company by the Bureau of Labor Statistics[11] shows that changeover to electronic data processing reduced the percentage of employees in low-medium wage categories from 91 percent to 73 percent. At the same time, the proportion in higher-paid levels increased from 8 percent to 27 percent. Using data from a small and a large insurance company, Helfgott[12] concludes that electronic data processing contributes to an upgrading of the office work force as many lower-level jobs are eliminated and the number of higher-level ones expanded. Empirical support for the hypothesis that computer technology increases the skill requirements in jobs remaining after conversion is also offered by Lee.[13]

The evidence indicates that electronic data-processing equipment generally upgrades part of the clerical work force, while almost no downgrading occurs. A common theme is that computers are best at performing the repetitive task formerly done manually. As routine jobs are diminished, electronic data processing creates higher-level jobs filled by personnel who variously contribute to the operation of the computer system. However, these references observing an upgrading of the occupational structure in the office do not systematically differentiate between nonmechanized, mechanized, and automated man-machine relationships. In addition to the supporting clerical work force performing nonmechanized tasks, establishment of an electronic data-

---

11. U.S. Department of Labor, Bureau of Labor Statistics, *Studies on Automatic Technology: Number 2—The Introduction of an Electronic Computer in a Large Insurance Company* (Washington, D.C.: U.S. Government Printing Office, 1955).
12. Roy B. Helfgott, "EDP and the Office Work Force," *Industrial and Labor Relations Review,* 19 (July 1966), p. 509.
13. H. C. Lee, "Electronic Data Processing and Skill Requirements," *Personnel Administration,* 29 (May–June 1966), p. 50.

processing center requires computer console operators, programmers, systems analysts, key-punch operators, and various other machine-operating jobs connected with punched-card data-processing equipment. It is misleading to predict a general upgrading of the office work force when computerization involves extremely functionally specialized jobs like those of key-punchers at the one extreme and enlarged jobs, such as systems analysts, at the other. The remainder of this chapter attempts to show the differential impact of computerization on office jobs.

COMPUTERS AND THE DIVISION OF LABOR: THE UP-GRADING EFFECT AMONG NONMECHANIZED OFFICE EMPLOYEES

Computer technology decreases the division of labor in nonmechanized clerical jobs as routine and repetitious jobs are eliminated. In addition to the studies cited earlier, Craig found an upgrading of job content and skills in a commercial department of a large insurance company during conversion to electronic accounting. In 1950, 87 percent of the jobs in this department had been in grades 1, 2, and 3, while only 63 percent were in those levels after conversion. The proportion of jobs in grades 4, 5, and 6 increased from 4 percent to 25 percent.[14] Rico reports a stepped-up need for coders, control clerks, and other clerks whose jobs involve a wider variety of tasks.[15]

In a study of the life insurance industry Whisler and Meyer[16] found that, contrary to their expectations, the

14. Harold F. Craig, *Administering a Conversion to Electronic Accounting* (Boston: Division of Research, Graduate School of Business Administration, Harvard University, 1955), p. 70.
15. Rico, "The Staffing Process and the Computer."
16. Thomas L. Whisler and Harold Meyer, *The Impact of EDP on Life Company Organization* (New York: Life Office Manage-

overwhelming impact of computerization was an upgrading of clerical skills in EDP-affected departments. Mann and Williams studied the changeover to electronic data processing in a large utility company. That computerization did not increase the division of labor in nonmechanized jobs is reflected in the fact that a 50 percent reduction in the number of jobs occurred in the central accounting area. Moreover, with the disclaimer that job enlargement is not a necessary concomitant of electronic data processing, Mann and Williams report that in this particular case "the work of the non-mechanized accounting groups responsible for the steps preparatory to machine processing was consolidated into a station arrangement with each member trained to handle five operations previously formed separately." [17] Mann and Williams also report that employees in jobs highly integrated with the computer indicated that their new jobs carried more responsibility, permitted a greater amount of variety and change, and provided expanded opportunities to learn new things. In general, they viewed their jobs as more important than the ones previously held.[18]

Another example of a decrease in the division of labor in nonmechanized jobs as as result of computerization is provided by the bank included in the present study. Before electronic data processing, posting for personal and business checking accounts was done by posting-machine operators. Posting formerly done by individual

ment Association, Personnel Administration Report, No. 34, 1967), p. 94.

17. Floyd C. Mann and Lawrence K. Williams, "Organizational Impact of White Collar Automation," *Annual Proceedings,* Industrial Relations Research Association (December 1958), p. 66.

18. Floyd C. Mann and Lawrence K. Williams, "Some Effects of the Changing Work Environment in the Office," *Journal of Social Issues,* 18 (July 1962), p. 95.

machine operators is presently a computer function, an excellent illustration of the absorption of repetitive tasks by computers. The redesign of posting-machine-operating jobs involved assigning each account control clerk to a "drum" of accounts, divided on the basis of the alphabet. Each account control clerk is responsible for and performs all operations bearing on her set of accounts. Their functions include inspecting daily computer output, updating checking accounts, and being alert for checks with old dates, forgeries, over-drafts, and so on. They also answer questions regarding accounts put to them by phone. Taking some action is part of their job, as for example calling a bank branch manager to see if an overdraft in one of his customer's accounts should be honored or payment stopped.

TECHNOLOGY AND DIVISION OF LABOR: MECHANIZATION IN THE OFFICE

Computer technology tends to absorb repetitious manual tasks and upgrade clerical jobs outside the electronic data-processing unit. But what are the effects within the electronic data complex itself? It is on this question that research is the most deficient in that the man-machine relationships accompanying punched-card mechaniza-tion and computer automation are not clearly distin-guished.

The type of mechanization underlying the punched-card system of data processing has profoundly affected the nature of clerical work. It was pointed out earlier that specialization of function had already begun to develop prior to this stage of mechanization due to the increase in the volume of data processed by offices. This tendency toward job specialization has been said to reach revolutionary proportions, however, as increas-ing numbers of office employees became operators of special-purpose machines as their sole function. The following passage captures this change:

In the past one employee may have been entrusted with an entire bookkeeping and recording operation; where the same operation is performed on punched-card machines several employees may be needed for different parts of the job—a supervisor to decide how the operation will be done, a key-punch operator to punch the cards, and operators in charge of feeding the cards into the sorting machines, tabulators, etc.[19]

With this increase in the division of labor, machine-operating jobs tend to take on the characteristics of monotony and repetitiveness long attached to much of factory work. For example, job descriptions indicate that the interests of a sorting-machine operator should be a "preference for activities of a routine, organized nature to perform repetitive tasks of tending [a] machine" and he should have the "ability to work under specified instructions with little independent action involved." Similarly, a key-punch operator should have a "preference for organized and routine activities to transfer data onto punch cards," be "able to perform repetitive duties of operating [a] key-punch machine," and have the "ability to follow instructions and set procedures to transfer data onto punch cards." [20]

The most recent stage of technological development, computerization, is linked with the punched-card mode of data processing. Rather than totally supplanting the punched-card system, electronic data-processing technology makes use of certain of these machines for input and output functions. For this reason all employees in an electronic data-processing unit are not experiencing

---

19. "Effects of Mechanisation and Automation in Offices: II,"
p. 266.
20. U.S. Department of Labor, Bureau of Employment Security, *Occupations in Electronic Computing Systems* (Washington, D.C.: U.S. Government Printing Office, 1965), pp. 30, 42.

automation; some work in a system that is identical to
the mechanization of information processing. Employees
manning machines auxiliary to the computer(s), such
as key-punchers, collators, sorters, and so forth, are
semiskilled operators of special-purpose machines.
Computer technology, in this way, promotes job specialization. Hoos observed that functional specialization
similar to that experienced in the factory is being felt
by operators manning machines peripheral to the computer.[21]

Hoos[22] warns that it is a mistake to assume that all
office jobs before automation were interesting and that
all jobs related to electronic data processing are dull.
However, her data indicate that machine operators
found their previous jobs more interesting since they
performed a wider variety of tasks, such as filing, checking, posting, or typing. Their new jobs were simplified,
requiring both accuracy and speed. Deprived of freedom
of movement about the office and interaction with
other employees or customers, the key-punch operators
felt they were chained to their machines. Hoos sees little
to choose between key-punch operators and assembly-
line workers—it is her observation that this segment of
the office has become a "paper processing factory."
Functional specialization, production deadlines, easy
detection of errors, shift work, and machine noise all
contribute to this analogy.

Another study relates to the question of downgrading
among mechanized jobs in automated offices. Weber[23]

---

21. Ida R. Hoos, *Automation in the Office* (Washington, D.C.:
Public Affairs Press, 1961), pp. 68–69.
22. Ida R. Hoos, "When the Computer Takes Over the Office,"
Harvard Business Review, 38 (July–August 1960), p. 104.
23. C. Edward Weber, "Impact of Electronic Data Processing on
Clerical Skills," *Personnel Administration,* 22–33 (January–
February 1959), pp. 20–26.

compared clerical workers in nonmechanized jobs with employees in the tabulating and computing departments of a fabricating plant and nonmechanized clerical workers with employees in the tabulating department of a steelworks. In both plants a larger proportion of employees in mechanized departments were concentrated in lower job grades than were clerks in nonmechanized departments. For example, in the steelworks 32 percent of the clerks in cost accounting were in the bottom two job grades compared with 80 percent in these lower job grades for those in the tabulating department. Cost accounting had 41 percent of its people in the highest job grade, while the tabulating department had only 11 percent in this grade. In the steel plant office, routine work was eliminated in the accounting department, but routine jobs (operation of keypunch machines and tabulating machines) were added in the tabulating department.

Contrary to the evidence just cited, some have argued that office automation has not produced upgrading and that a reduction in skill requirements is often the case. For example, Hoos's findings agree with Bright's[24] observations regarding factory workers that skill requirements in the office are not directly proportional to increases in automation. Hoos contends that the dull, repetitive, and low-paying jobs eliminated by automation are being offset by machine-operating jobs that are no less dull, repetitive, and financially unrewarding.[25] While conceding that factory automation may produce job enlargement as functions are integrated, Hoos feels that office automation, by contrast, severely

---

24. James R. Bright, "Does Automation Raise Skill Requirements?" *Harvard Business Review*, 36 (July–August 1958), p. 98.
25. Hoos, "When the Computer Takes Over the Office," p. 105.

splinters job content.[26] Similarly, Sola[27] asserts that job enlargement is possible in the case of a former punch-press operator whose new job in an automated factory involves monitoring several automatic punch and drill presses. On the other hand, Sola contends, a narrowing of job content is associated with automated technology in the office. A clerk performing a number of tasks is most likely experiencing his or her peak in job size. New jobs created by the installation of electronic processing are, in this view, those of operating special-purpose machines such as key-punches, collators, and sorters.

It is important to note that job specialization was experienced by employees operating equipment peripheral to the computer. Jobs of this kind illustrate a mechanized man-machine relationship rather than an automated one.[28] It is a mistake to assume that the mechanized man-machine relationship associated with the punched-card system of data processing is the final one in the development of office technology.

COMPUTERS AND DIVISION OF LABOR: COMPUTER OPERATORS AND COMPUTER SOFTWARE PERSONNEL

Computer Operators
It has already been observed that computer technology

---

26. Hoos, *Automation in the Office,* p. 125.
27. F. C. Sola, "Personnel Administration and Office Automation: A Review of Empirical Research," *ILR Research,* 8 (1962), p. 5.
28. For further discussion of job specialization as a characteristic of peripheral machine-operating jobs in electronic data-processing centers, see "Effects of Mechanisation and Automation in Offices: II"; "Effects of Mechanisation and Automation in Offices: III," *International Labor Review,* 81 (April 1960), pp. 350–369; J. R. Dale, *The Clerk in Industry* (Liverpool University Press, 1962), pp. 83–90; Leonard Rico, *The Advance Against Paperwork* (Ann Arbor: University of Michigan Press, 1967).

spurs the demand for higher-level personnel. Within
the electronic data-processing unit, a need is created
for systems analysts, programmers, and console operators.
A study by the Bureau of Labor Statistics[29] compared
the grade status of employees before transfer to positions
in electronic data processing with their level after transfer. Almost 83 percent were promoted to higher grade
levels, 17 percent remained at the same grade level, and
less than 1 percent experienced downgrading.

Of particular interest in this context is the automated
man-machine relationship in the office represented by
the computer operator. In the automated offices surveyed
by the Bureau of Labor Statistics, console operators,
along with programmers and systems analysts, were at
the top of the salary structure. Two factors, mental
ability and responsibility for performance, contributed
the majority of total points that determined the grade
and pay level of console operators in the evaluation
system of one large company.[30] In another study, a
computer had been installed into a department that
had formerly done clerical and statistical work using
punched-card equipment. Computer operators were the
only employees who were upgraded.[31] Required attributes of a computer operator include capacity for responsibility, the ability to comprehend complex technology, and initiative and judgment in meeting periodic
emergencies.[32]

There are at least two ways in which automated

---

29. *Adjustments to the Introduction of Office Automation,* p. 57.
30. *Ibid.,* p. 40.
31. K. G. Van Auken, Jr., "A Case Study of the Impact of Automation on Skills and Equipment," in *Man and Automation,* The
Technology Project (New Haven, Conn.: Yale University Press,
1956), pp. 30–31.
32. H. De Bivort, "Automation—Some Social Aspects," *International Labor Review,* 72 (December 1955), p. 486.

technology reduces functional specialization. First, it is clear from the literature that the nonmechanized clerical jobs most often replaced by the computer are those routine and repetitious in nature. An upgrading of the clerical labor force as a result of automation is the predominant observation in reported research. Second, and more important in this context, as automation advances, the once-separate functions performed by auxiliary machine operators will be increasingly integrated into the computer controlled system:

Improvements in data input and output procedures will undoubtedly eliminate the peripheral processing operations. The printing out of information coming from the computer, for example, is increasingly tied directly into the computer system so that an operator of separate printing equipment is no longer necessary. This example of elimination of a functionally specialized task through the integration of production processes is a direct equivalent of the effects of factory automation. . . .[33]

As a result of the integration of formerly discrete steps in the processing of data, the growth rate of non-computer-machine-operating jobs will decline. In two of the most highly automated industries, insurance and the federal government, advances in computer technology are expected to turn downward the growth rate of key-punch-operating jobs.[34] More marked decreases are expected among electric accounting-machine operators in insurance, the federal government, and banking.[35]

---

33. William A. Faunce, "Automation and the Division of Labor," *Social Problems*, 13 (Fall 1965), p. 158.
34. *Technological Trends in Major American Industries,* pp. 252, 258.
35. Rose Wiener, "Changing Manpower Requirements in Banking," *Monthly Labor Review*, 85 (September 1962), p. 905. The banking industry, due to the processing of checks, shows an increase in some machine-operating jobs such as reader-sorter operators and check-proof-encoding machine operators, in spite of increased computerization.

In insurance, for example, "these card tabulating departments, which have existed in some insurance companies for decades, will soon be virtually eliminated from the industry." [36] A similar trend appeared in the companies included in the present study. After the installation of advanced computers (IBM 360 series), the number of key-punch operators and tabulating personnel decreased slightly in each firm. Increases occurred among computer operators, programmers, and systems analysts.

It seems evident that the demand for computer operators and computer software personnel will continue to increase substantially. And computer operators have larger jobs in the sense that they are responsible for a computer installation that has absorbed functions performed separately (either by employees in nonmechanized clerical jobs or by special-purpose machine operators within and outside the supporting punched-card unit) prior to being integrated into the computer system.

The integration or consolidation of separate files and functions is being promoted by computer manufacturers and increasingly adopted as a goal by companies with computers. The large insurance company participating in the present research provides a concrete example of integration. Before installing computers this company had five separate organizational units containing machines characteristic of punched-card data-processing systems. Currently, they have only one such installation. Prior to the integration of data into master files, a capability permitted by computer technology, the handling of a single insurance policy might have required as many as forty cards scattered throughout the organization. Just over a decade ago it may have taken

---

36. *Technological Trends in Major American Industries,* p. 253.

a week to obtain all the information on a single policy
because various cards were maintained and processed
at many different points throughout the company. That
integration or consolidation eliminates intermediate
manual and mechanical steps in data processing and
promotes a more continuous work flow is reflected in
this statement:

Before consolidation, many separate operating departments,
each having only a part of the policy file, were required to
handle a wide variety of insurance office functions from
premium billing to loan accounting. As each function is
programmed for EDP, it becomes possible to handle more
tasks through a single master policy record contained in
the computer file. Separate records and tabulating units
are eliminated, fewer controls and audits are required to
keep all policy information in balance, and clerical posting
jobs are greatly reduced.[37]

The computer operator's responsibilites are to mount
the appropriate tapes, avoid making errors, detect mistakes, and correct them when feasible. His skill lies in
the ability to make decisions when something goes
wrong; when the system runs smoothly, little skill is
required. Computer operators are given job specifications such as which tapes to mount and which code
number to type into the computer. But when something
goes wrong, the operator must know the system and do
the right thing. As among monitors in a continuous-
process production system, the computer operator's job
primarily involves responsibility for the proper functioning of the system.

Computer Software Personnel

Programmers and systems analysts perform "software"
functions that are essential to the development, change,
and operation of the hardware system. Systems analysts

---

37. *Ibid.,* p. 250.

are continuously developing and modifying the plans by which organizational functions may be programmed and handled by the computer system. On the basis of this plan, programmers write detailed instructions, called programs, which instruct the computer as to what operations it should perform. The period of training is longer and the minimum educational requirements are higher for both systems analysts and programmers compared to other types of nonsupervisory office employees. From a survey of 20 offices, the Bureau of Labor Statistics observes that with computerization the new positions of computer-console operator, programmer, and systems analysts are at the peak of the salary structure. Systems analysts and programmers ranked somewhat higher than console operators.[38]

Some observers view computer programmers and systems analysts as part of management.[39] If one considers only job grade and salary level, this conclusion appears justified. But the use of rank and salary as indicators is misleading. In the large insurance company participating in this study, programmers and systems analysts are in middle management in terms of salary level, but their actual duties are neither supervisory nor managerial. In fact, advanced computer operators, if placed by salary level, would also be classified as managerial. Clearly, personnel performing software functions are a new type of office employee, so new that confusion is created in attempting to place them in the conventional dichotomy of clerical versus managerial. Since the focus of this study is on the nature of work, it is most logical to consider their functions to be "clerical." They are, to be sure, a novel type of clerical employee, being one of

---

38. *Adjustments to the Introduction of Office Automation,* p. 40.
39. See Weber, "Impact of Electronic Data Processing on Clerical Skills"; and Rico, *The Advance Against Paperwork,* pp. 260–261.

the automated man-machine relationships created by
computer technology.

SUMMARY
At the beginning of this chapter, it was contended that
generalizations with regard to changes in job content
and skills of clerical employees as a result of technological change are often made without respect to variation
in man-machine relationships. An outline of the stages
of mechanization in the office was offered in order to
differentiate several man-machine relationships in the
office, roughly analogous to those found in the factory.
A point of view was developed on the impact of computerization on the nature of clerical work. Computers
tend to upgrade nonmechanized clerical, computer-
operating, and computer software jobs but at the same
time require highly specialized machine-operating jobs
for data preparation.
  Central to this chapter is the position that variations
in the effects of technology on office work may be masked
if distinctions are not made among nonmechanized,
mechanized, and automated man-machine relationships.
Having completed this framework, it remains to relate
empirically technology in the office to alienation.

In the preceding chapter stages of mechanization in the office were outlined and a position on the impact of technology on the nature of office work was developed. A summary of this framework precedes presentation of the findings.

Early mechanization in the office involved technological devices such as typewriters and adding machines that were used by employees as aids during the performance of their several functions. At first, skills were affected in only a minor way by these technological developments. Later, some of these rather simple mechanical devices were used for the mass production of information by machine operators (for example, the typing pool).

The next stage of mechanization in the office, punched-card data processing, greatly accelerated the trend toward functional specialization. Many more special-purpose machine-operating jobs evolved, placing employees filling these jobs in a relationship to technology similar to the mass-production factory worker. Work in these jobs is repetitive, mechanically paced, and minutely subdivided.

Computers constitute the most recent stage in the application of technology to paper processing. Computers tend to absorb routine and repetitive tasks performed by lower-level clerical personnel, while increasing the number of higher-level clerical jobs inside and outside of the electronic data-processing unit. Within the computer facility proper, the higher-level positions of computer operator, programmer, and systems analyst are created. At the same time the operation of an electronic data-processing system requires a host of employees who operate such special-purpose machines as key-punches, tabulators, sorters, collators, and interpreters. If these operating jobs exist in the organization before computers are introduced they may be reduced in number, but they are not eliminated. They are retained to perform data-preparation functions for the computer and to do jobs that are not computer-processed. For companies that skip the punched-card mode of data processing as a distinct stage of technological development and move directly into computers, machine-operating jobs associated with the punched-card system are introduced for the first time. Automated technology, then, has the effect of increasing as well as decreasing functional specialization.

From this review of research findings it is possible to posit for the office a relationship between the phases in the man-machine relationship and degree of functional specialization analogous to that found in the factory. That is, what are termed traditional nonmechanized clerical jobs (that is, secretaries and clerks of all kinds and levels) have less functionally specialized jobs than do office employees in mechanized or special-purpose machine-operating jobs (for example, production typing and key-punch operating). Division of labor is again less specialized in both hardware (computer operators) and software (computer programmers and systems analysts) man-machine relationships created by computers. The remainder of this chapter is devoted to relating empirically these phases in the man-machine relationship in the office to alienation among office employees.

PHASES IN THE MAN-MACHINE RELATIONSHIP AND ALIENATION

Powerlessness in Work
The predicted curvilinear relationship between the phases in the man-machine relationship and powerless-

ness in work did appear among office workers. However, Table 5.1 shows that the relationship tends to be positive in direction until computer software personnel are considered. A sense of powerlessness increases slightly as technology reaches higher levels up to and including computer operators. However, significance tests between percentages did not reveal any differences among the three types of office workers at the .05 level or above.[1] But while 53 percent of the nonmechanized clerks, 58 percent of the office machine operators, and 61 percent of the computer operators were above the median on the Powerlessness scale, only 9 percent of the programmers and systems analysts experienced a lack of freedom and control in their jobs at a similar level. It is also evident in Table 5.1 that programmers and systems analysts have nearly the same percentage above the Powerlessness scale median (9 and 8 percent, respectively). Percentage differences among more traditional clerks, office machine operators, and computer operators are not sufficiently large to draw any distinctions regarding the level of freedom and control each category felt they exercised at work.

  Programmers and systems analysts have been labeled

---

1. References to whether percentage differences are statistically significant are based on t tests of the significance of differences between percentages. Strictly speaking, this statistical test is to be applied to random samples, which part of the white-collar sample in this study is not. An alternative would have been to choose arbitrarily a percentage spread, like 10 percent, and interpret a difference of this size as being "real." The decision was made to rely on t tests, with full awareness of the violation of the randomness assumption, rather than choose an arbitrary percentage difference. In nearly all instances percentage differences said to be significantly different as a result of a t test were of the order of 10 percent or more. In many cases differences exceeding 10 percent were necessary for the differences to be judged as statistically significant.

Table 5.1
Percentage above the Median on the Scale of Powerlessness in Work by Phases in the Man-Machine Relationship for the Total Sample, Males and Females

| | Phases in the Man-Machine Relationship | | | | | |
| | | | Automated | | | |
Powerlessness in Work Scale	Non-mechanized	Mechanized (EDP and Non-EDP)	(Computer Operators)	(Computer Software Combined)	Program-mers	Systems Analysts
Total Sample above Median	53% (464)	58% (281)	61% (73)	9% (18)[a]	9% (15)	8% (3)
Males above Median	42 (26)	50 (31)	62 (73)	7 (9)[b]		
Females above Median	53 (438)	59 (250)	—[c]	12 (9)[d]		

[a] $X^2 = 157.40$, $df = 4$, $P < .001$, $\overline{C} = .40$
[b] $X^2 = 93.96$, $df = 4$, $P < .001$, $\overline{C} = .62$
[c] Since there were only two female computer operators, they have been excluded from this part of the analysis.
[d] $X^2 = 53.15$, $df = 4$, $P < .001$, $\overline{C} = .27$

the new elite in the computerized office; they are at
the top of clerical occupational structure.[2] It would be
expected that their level of alienation is lower than
for other nonsupervisory office employees. Some description of the work situation among computer software
personnel will make it clear why they are less separated
from the exercise of freedom and control on the job
than other types of office workers. Both programmers
and systems analysts can to a considerable extent vary
the steps by which they accomplish their tasks. Systems
analysts perform their function under few parameters.
A systems analyst obtains information about an operation
to be computerized through consultation with the user
and direct observation of the work. On the basis of the
understanding gained, he proceeds to design a workable
system on his own. Translation of written instructions
to computer applicability by programmers is also done
with a great deal of discretion. Perhaps to make a point,
the head of one software department made the statement that the same problem, if given to six different
programmers, will produce six different answers.

Neither programmers nor systems analysts are restricted
to a particular working area. A systems analyst confers
with a user at the conceptual level and then spends a
great deal of time at his desk working out a design.
Programmers meet with users, deliver jobs to the

---

2. See Ida R. Hoos, "When the Computer Takes Over the Office,"
Harvard Business Review, 38 (July 1960), p. 103; "Effects of Mechanisation and Automation in Offices: II," *International Labour
Review*, 81 (March 1960), pp. 258–259; K. G. Van Auken, Jr.,
"A Case Study of the Impact of Automation on Skills and Equipment," in *Man and Automation* (New Haven, Conn.: Yale University Press, 1956), p. 31; and U.S. Department of Labor, Bureau
of Labor Statistics, Bulletin Number 1241, *Automation and Employment Opportunities for Office Workers* (Washington, D.C.:
U.S. Government Printing Office, 1958), p. 8.

computer, and consult with their project leader on a given job. It was estimated by one software executive that programmers spend as much as 40 percent of their time away from their desks.

Control over the amount of work produced is heavily vested with software personnel. On any given assignment the programmer and his supervisor together often determine the time it should take to write the program, which may vary from two hours to six months. Among systems analysts there is even less of a superimposed time frame for the completion of a systems design. Closeness of supervision varies with the time one has been programming or designing systems. During the first six months supervision is likely to be fairly close. After a couple of years the work of a programmer or systems analysts will probably not undergo scrunity.

It appears that some factors impinging on nonmechanized clerical and computer-operating jobs may override the effect of job size with respect to powerlessness in work. Clerical workers in nonmechanized jobs did have a slightly smaller percentage high on the Powerlessness Scale than machine-operating office workers, but the difference was not as marked as had been expected. Several factors may account for this finding. First, the highly interdependent flow of work between data preparation and computer processing is a possible contributor. With respect to powerlessness, the demands of the computer may have exercised a similar effect on both mechanized and nonmechanized clerical jobs. Though not directly subject to the demands of a machine, as in the case of machine operators, many clerks in a computerized company are tied to the input and output cycles of the computer system. Work done on one day must be fed into the computer for updating, and computer output is necessary for the performance of daily tasks. Of course, clerical jobs are differentially affected by computers, some more than others, depending on how closely the jobs are linked to the computer system. The design of this study did not permit dividing the sample of nonmechanized clerical workers in terms of the degree to which their jobs are geared to the computer.

Second, business volume is increasing dramatically in computerized organizations. Part of this is due to the expansion that computers make possible; part of it is due to economic forces in the larger society. Whatever the source, the dramatic increase in the volume of information to be processed tends to place heavier work loads on nonmechanized clerical employees.

Third, rapid growth in white-collar employment tends to create a tight labor market, leaving offices short of the number of employees they need. All of these factors, interdependence of functions, increase in business volume, and labor shortage, probably operate to diminish the freedom and control of nonmechanized clerical workers.

The conclusion that clerical workers holding non-mechanized jobs experience less freedom and control than would be predicted on the basis of the intrinsic nature of their jobs is supported by Lee's study.[3] Clerks in a shoe manufacturing firm that had just installed a large-scale computer reported that the variety of tasks they were required to perform had increased after the installation. In other words, job specialization had decreased. Still, these same clerical employees felt that deadlines had increased in number, that their freedom and flexibility in choice of work methods had diminished, and that their ability to control the speed and sequence of their work had been reduced.

---

3. H. C. Lee, "Do Workers Really Want More Flexibility on the Job?" *Personnel*, 42 (March–April 1965), pp. 76–77.

An interview with the assistant manager of a non-mechanized clerical department in the large insurance company is also consistent with Lee's findings. He reported that the shortage of workers overburdened the existing employee complement, that supervision had to be close, that deadlines were stringent, and that the volume of work was currently enormous and constantly expanding. Employees were not free to move away from their desks except during regular breaks and even then were asked not to leave the immediate area. Regimentation is evidenced by the fact that bells signaled when to start work, when to take breaks, when to go to and return from lunch, and when to end the day. Employees could suggest alterations in data forms and work flow to supervisors but could not make any changes without supervisory approval.

Nonmechanized clerical employees in this company, however, were not subject to the steady pressure placed on office workers in mechanized jobs. The work load of nonmechanized clerks varies from day to day. Mondays and Thursdays were their busiest days, but they could normally work at a slower pace on the other three work days. If the mail receipt on a given day is heavy or if a heavy backlog existed, their freedom and control was diminished whatever the day of the week.

A more surprising finding was that computer operators had a slightly larger percentage (61 percent) high on the Powerlessness Scale than office employees in either mechanized or nonmechanized jobs. There is a sign just inside the computer room of the large insurance company bearing this message: "The tolerance for error is zero." One gets a clue from this declaration that in a computer facility predictability and precisely timed routines have a higher value than operator freedom and control. It is known that the computer is the source of work deadlines and determines the work pace in jobs related to preliminary data preparation. Computer operators apparently are not immune to the demands of the technology. The bulk of a computer operator's job is spent on production, that is, on the running of jobs, and while on production time, control and freedom are quite limited. Computer operators must adhere to the predetermined schedule of jobs in order to meet the delivery time set for a work unit's output. Failure to get information out of the computer on time costs the company unproductive man-hours. Deadline pressures for the most part rule out any variation in the daily production schedule. Only senior operators exercise control in handling emergencies and changing the schedule.

In contrast, a portion of a computer operator's day may be consumed by "debugging" or running untried programs through the computer for an operational check. On debugging jobs more initiative is permitted the operator. Normally, however, only a small amount of time is spent off production in this type of less-structured work.

Console-operating procedures are clearly laid out, and operators work from detailed written instructions. The machinery is so expensive that operators are discouraged from experimenting or solving operating problems. The division of labor between computer operators and programmers is rather rigidly honored. Computer operators are expected to follow programming specifications and are discouraged from changing a program. Operators with a desire and propensity for programming may enter the software side of the operation, but not while they are operating a computer. Should a computer run stop, operators are not normally expected to make a correction. One manager characterized computer operators as human warning lights—they must report to a supervisor or programmer if a computer run aborts.

An operator may decide to rerun a job on the assumption that a mechanical failure has occurred. However, computer downtime is easily traceable. Since each operator must keep an exact log of the uses to which this time on the computer is put, he will probably feel constrained not to risk wasting costly computer time. The following statement by an EDP manager makes this point, though it should be taken more for the philosophy it reflects rather than for its accuracy: "A computer operator who can save one minute of operating time will make his pay for the month."

Movement from the immediate working area is restricted among computer operators since it is not wise to leave such expensive and complicated machinery unattended. In at least one insurance company in this study, computer operators cannot leave the computer room for coffee. Leaving the room for more pressing needs requires getting another operator to cover in the interim. Supervision of computer operators is close, not in the physical sense but in the sense that job order is predetermined, methods and procedures are minutely outlined, and operators must report to a supervisor in the event of a malfunction whose source is not immediately apparent.[4]

Only males were included in the blue-collar sample. Females, on the other hand, comprise the bulk of the clerical labor force, in general, and the present sample, in particular, except for computer operators, programmers, and systems analysts. Consequently, the relationship between the phases in the man-machine relationship

---

4. Individual items included in the Powerlessness scale were examined in order to see if any variations in the proportions high on any single aspect of powerlessness appeared. Only on the supervision item ("To what extent are you free from close supervision while doing your job?") were computer operators less alienated than nonmechanized and machine-operating office workers.

and powerlessness in work was examined for males and females separately. Table 5.1 contains the answers to two questions. First, does the same pattern of relationship between technology and powerlessness appear among both males and females? Second, are males and females in like man-machine relationships significantly different in attitude?

Among males the trend is the same as in the case of the total sample. Lack of freedom and control on the job was not much more prevalent among male employees in nonmechanized jobs than among those operating machines (42 percent versus 50 percent), and the latter were not significantly different on powerlessness than were computer operators. The difference between computer operators (62 percent) and males in nonmechanized jobs (42 percent) was significant at the .01 level. Male computer software personnel were significantly less alienated than male employees in the other three man-machine relationships.

Females in nonmachine operating jobs were not significantly lower in terms of powerlessness than those operating machines on a full-time basis (53 percent versus 59 percent). Since only two of the computer operators were female, they have been excluded in all comparisons between the sexes. Female programmers and systems analysts, like their male counterparts, are significantly less alienated than females in machine and nonmachine operating jobs.

A second comparison to be made is between males and females in each man-machine relationship in terms of percentages above the median on the Powerlessness scale. No significant differences appeared between males and females performing nonmechanized clerical tasks, operating machines, or performing software functions. In sum, sexual differences did not substantially alter the pattern found for the total sample, and males and females in the same man-machine relationship did not respond in any significantly different way on the Powerlessness scale.

Though it does not appear in Table 5.1, it is interesting to note that EDP machine operators[5] did not have a much larger percentage high on the Powerlessness scale than did non-EDP machine operators (59 percent versus 57 percent). Even without the pressure of the computer, over half of the non-EDP machine operators were above the median on the scale of Powerlessness in work.

Meaninglessness in Work

Meaninglessness in work is more clearly related to the degree of functional specialization than either powerlessness or normlessness. An important assumption is that the larger the scope of the job, the greater will be the jobholder's perception of how his work is related to the jobs of workmates, to work done in other departments, and to the products of the larger organization. It seems obvious that with growth in organizational size a sense of meaninglessness is likely to increase whether or not work is highly subdivided. Functional specialization, however, further contributes to the worker's sense of unrelatedness to the work of others regardless of company size.

It can be seen in Table 5.2 that the predicted curvilinear relationship between the phases in the man-machine relationship and meaninglessness in work was significant at the .001 level for the total sample. Further specification is obtained by examining percentage differences. Fifty-two percent of the clerical employees

---

5. Throughout this chapter, EDP machine operators refers to punched-card machine operators such as key-punch and card-sorter operators. Computer operators will always be designated as such.

Table 5.2
Percentage above the Median on the Scale of Meaninglessness in Work by Phases in the Man-Machine Relationship for the Total Sample, Males and Females

Meaninglessness in Work Scale	Phases in the Man-Machine Relationship					
			Automated			
	Non-mechanized	Mechanized (EDP and Non-EDP)	(Computer Operators)	(Computer Software Personnel Combined)	Programmers	Systems Analysts
Total Sample above Median	53% (496)	63% (329)	48% (59)	34% (73)[a]	41% (69)	10% (4)
Males above Median	44 (28)	65 (43)	48 (57)	30 (41)[b]		
Females above Median	55 (468)	62 (286)	—[c]	44 (32)[d]		

[a] $X^2 = 50.45$, $df = 4$, $P < .001$, $\overline{C} = .22$
[b] $X^2 = 24.49$, $df = 4$, $P < .001$, $\overline{C} = .33$
[c] Since there were only two female computer operators, they have been excluded from this part of the analysis.
[d] $X^2 = 17.32$, $df = 4$, $P < .01$, $\overline{C} = .15$

in nonmechanized jobs were above the median on the Meaninglessness scale as were 48 percent of the computer operators. The level of meaninglessness was essentially the same for employees in the nonmechanized and automated categories. A larger percentage of employees in the mechanized man-machine relationship were high on the Meaninglessness scale (63 percent). This percentage was significantly higher than for employees in both nonmechanized ($P < .001$) and computer-operating jobs ($P < .01$).

The lack of a sense of interrelatedness of their job to the work of others was significantly lower among programmers and systems analysts than among other office employees. Thirty-four percent of the software personnel were above the median on the Meaninglessness scale compared to 48 percent of the traditional clerks ($P < .001$), 63 percent of the office machine operators, and 48 percent of the computer operators. Not unexpectedly, programmers had a lower sense of meaning than did systems analysts (41 percent versus 10 percent). The job title "systems analyst" connotes the fact that one in this position would, as part of his function, have to develop a keen sense of the interrelationship of functions and jobs.

Considering the male subsample alone, precisely the same set of relationships obtained as in the total sample. That is, males in nonmechanized and computer-operating positions were quite similar in terms of a lack of a sense of relatedness of their work to that of others; office employees engaged in mechanized-type jobs had a significantly ($P < .05$) larger proportion above the Meaninglessness scale median than those in either of the other two man-machine relationships; and computer software personnel exhibited the lowest level of meaninglessness of all. Females in the nonmechanized worker-technology relationship had a lower percentage above the median ($P < .01$) than was the case for female office machine operators.

The expectation that the responses of males and females to the same types of work might be different was generally not upheld. Percentages above the median on the Meaninglessness scale were not significantly higher for males in nonmechanized and mechanized jobs than for females with similar relationships to technology at work. The one exception is that females in computer software positions are more alienated than males in these kinds of jobs ($P < .05$).

It does not appear in Table 5.2, but, as in the case of powerlessness, non-EDP machine operators were not significantly different from EDP-related machine operators. Sixty-one percent of the stenographers, typists, and other non-EDP machine operators were above the median on the Meaninglessness scale, as were 65 percent of the punched-card machine operators.

Normlessness at Work

Several writers have observed that mechanization and computerization promote a leveling of the office occupational structure.[6] This is especially clear in that seg-

---

6. Enid Mumford and Olive Banks, *The Computer and the Clerk* (London: Routledge and Kegan Paul, 1967); A. Kushner, "People and Computers," *Personnel* (January–February 1963), pp. 27–34; Albert Blum, "Computers and Clerical Workers" (Oberhausen, Germany: Document of the Third International Conference on Rationalization, Automation and Technological Change, sponsored by the Metalworkers' Industrial Union of the Federal Republic of Germany, 1968); Leonard Rico, *The Advance Against Paperwork* (Ann Arbor, Michigan: Bureau of Industrial Relations, Graduate School of Business Administration, University of Michigan, 1967), pp. 286–292; and Leonora Stettner, "Survey of Literature on Social and Economic Effects of Technical Change," in Jack Stieber, editor, *Employment Problems of Automation and Advanced Technology: An International Perspective* (London: Macmillan, 1966), pp. 451–479.

ment of the occupational structure comprised of office machine operators:

Whereas in the early offices employees could look forward to moving ahead gradually through a series of well recognized steps, towards higher-grade jobs, nowadays in large, mechanized offices the intermediary steps have vanished, as the work formerly done by semi-skilled clerks is performed on machines. . . . In many cases unskilled workers are employed for . . . subordinate tasks, and they are simply given brief training on the job and have little chance of acquiring enough experience of the whole work process to be promoted to the executive or supervisory levels. They thus often suffer a double sense of frustration through this excessive compartmentalization of functions—not only is their job content too limited to afford any sense of accomplishment but in addition they have often the feeling of being "stuck" in a particular job with very little opportunity to move ahead.[7]

One expected consequence of a truncated occupational structure is the realistic assessment on the part of employees that upward mobility is not likely for them in that structure. It is reasonable to assume that among people working in an occupational hierarchy too flat for advancement one response will be to feel that promotions are achieved in the company on grounds other than merit or ability.[8] Placing blame on other individuals or the "system" rather than on oneself is a common human response.

It was predicted that the extreme job specialization experienced by office employees in mechanized jobs would promote in them a greater sense of normlessness

---

7. "Effects of Mechanisation and Automation in Offices: II," *International Labour Review,* 81 (March 1960), p. 267.
8. This was apparently the case among automobile workers in Chinoy's study. See Ely Chinoy, *Automobile Workers and the American Dream* (Garden City, N.Y.: Doubleday & Company, Inc. 1955).

Table 5.3
Percentage above the Median on the Scale of Normlessness at Work by Phases in the Man-Machine Relationship for the Total Sample, Males and Females

	Phases in the Man-Machine Relationship					
			Automated			
Normlessness at Work Scale	Non-mechanized	Mechanized (EDP and Non-EDP)	(Computer Operators)	(Computer Software Personnel Combined)	Programmers	Systems Analysts
Total Sample above Median	49% (461)	49% (255)	34% (41)	37% (77)[a]	39% (65)	31% (12)
Males above Median	45 (29)	56 (36)	34 (40)	30 (42)[b]		
Females above Median	50 (432)	52 (219)	—[c]	52 (35)[d]		

[a] $X^2 = 23.40$, $df = 4$, $P < .001$, $\bar{C} = .15$
[b] $X^2 = 14.94$, $df = 4$, $P < .02$, $\bar{C} = .26$
[c] Since there were only two female computer operators, they have been excluded from this part of the analysis.
[d] N. S

than would exist among non-machine-operating clerks. Contrary to expectation, an equal proportion (49 percent) of clerks and office machine operators were above the median on the Normlessness scale (Table 5.3). This finding raises the possibility that technology affects the clerical occupational structure, to be differentiated from the intrinsic nature of the job, in a direction thought to occur primarily among the machine-operating segment. Clerical employees holding nonmechanized jobs in computerized organizations may, like office machine operators, be denied a sense of upward occupational movement for two interrelated reasons. First, the elimination of lower-level jobs reduces the number of job levels through which office workers may pass. Second, and at the other extreme of the skill ladder, many of the higher-level positions created by computerization are not within reach of most clerical workers. On-the-job experience, whether it be key-punching or checking forms, does not prepare one for the technical tasks performed by a computer operator, programmer, or systems analyst. The promotion of clerks into any one of these higher-level jobs created by computerization is based on special training and aptitude, not on knowledge and experience gained on the job. It is more likely that clerks could become computer operators than programmers or systems analysts. Requirements for a computer-operating position are not as stringent as in the case of programmers and systems analysts. However, this may change as computer installations become more complex and sophisticated. For example, the minimum educational level for a computer operator in the large insurance company in the present study is two years of college.

To the extent that these changes occur, a gap in the office occupational hierarchy is opened. With the gradual removal of middle rungs, upward mobility will be increasingly blocked for clerical employees. Opportunity to start at the bottom and work up may be diminished for nonmechanized clerks as well as for office machine operators. A sense of normlessness may develop among the non-machine-operating segment of the clerical labor force even though their jobs are not minutely subdivided.

The conclusion that machine-operating and non-machine-operating office employees are not different with respect to perceived inability to advance in the company on the basis of merit is indirectly supported by other research on automation in the office. Mumford and Banks[9] found that male bank clerks who before computerization were sanguine about their advancement possibilities were more pessimistic after the conversion. In an earlier conversion study, Hardin[10] found that among clerks in computer-affected departments outside the EDP unit a slightly higher percentage (17 percent) reported a perceived decrease in promotion chances compared with clerks in the computer area (4 percent) and with clerks in unaffected departments (2 percent). In a large utility company converting to computers, Mann and Williams report a 50 percent reduction in the number of jobs after installation. Elimination of clerical jobs left an occupational structure with fewer grade levels. Employees subject to this change felt that opportunities for promotion were less than before computerization. Mann and Williams sum it up this way:

The removal of many middle level decision-making jobs . . . means that there is less opportunity for progression

---

9. Mumford and Banks, *The Computer and the Clerk,* p. 186.
10. Einar Hardin, "The Reactions of Employees to Office Automation," *Monthly Labor Review,* 83 (September 1960), pp. 927–928. It should be noted that the majority of clerks felt that the computer would have no effect on their promotion chances.

in the organization. This has long been true for the assembly-line worker. The effect that such a promotion limit will have on the white-collar worker is unknown as yet, but it will probably disturb his illusion of mobility.[11]

A sense of inability to advance in the company on the basis of merit was not as prevalent among computer operators. The 34 percent of computer operators above the median on the Normlessness scale was significantly different ($P < .01$) from the 49 percent of machine-operating and non-machine-operating office workers high on this scale.

With respect to normlessness, systems analysts were not much different from programmers; 39 and 31 percent, respectively, were above the scale median. Combined, programmers and systems analysts were significantly lower on this dimension of alienation compared to clerks holding more traditional office jobs and office machine operators. Computer operators and software personnel were characterized by nearly the same level of alienation on the normlessness dimension (37 and 39 percent, respectively, were above the Normlessness scale median).

Table 5.3 shows that the pattern is somewhat different for females when men and women are examined separately. Fifty percent of the nonmechanized female clerks were above the median on the Normlessness scale, as were 52 percent of the female office machine operators. But because 52 percent of the female software employees are above the median, the curvilinear relationship does not hold. On the other hand, there was no significant difference between male machine operators and male

---

11. Floyd C. Mann and Lawrence K. Williams, "Organizational Impact of White-Collar Automation," *Annual Proceedings,* Industrial Relations Research Association (December 1958), p. 66.

clerks (45 percent versus 56 percent). Considering males alone, no significant difference appeared between non-mechanized clerks and computer operators. As in the total sample, both computer operators and computer software personnel are significantly lower on normlessness ($P < .01$) than male office machine operators.

Only one difference at a statistically reliable level appeared between males and females in each man-machine relationship for which comparable data were available. Females in computer software were significantly higher on normlessness than male programmers and systems analysts (52 versus 30 percent). This finding that females in computer software jobs feel more strongly than males that to advance they would have to engage in manipulation of some sort reflects a reality. Despite changes in recent years, when women, even in high-level positions such as programming and systems analyzing, look up the organizational ladder, they see males occupying the leadership positions.

Normlessness is the only alienation dimension on which a significant difference appeared between non-EDP and EDP machine operators. Forty-four percent of the non-EDP machine operators were above the median compared to 53 percent of the EDP-related machine operators ($P < .05$).[12]

Self-Evaluative Involvement
and Instrumental Work Orientation
In Chapter 3 the point was developed that jobs that deny workers freedom, control, meaning, and a sense of occupational progression based on merit and ability promote the withdrawal of ego from work and make work an instrument for the pursuit of goals and activities

---

12. These figures do not appear in Table 5.3.

outside of the work role. This idea was empirically examined and partially supported among factory workers. Though the difference was not statistically significant, a higher percentage of craftsmen were high on the scale of Self-Evaluative Involvement in work than were assemblers (48 percent versus 38 percent). Both craftsmen and assemblers were significantly lower in self-evaluative involvement than monitors working in a continuous-process plant. Seventy percent of the monitors were above the median on this scale.

A similar but less clear-cut pattern appeared among office employees (Table 5.4). The three-percentage-point spread (46 percent and 49 percent) between clerks in nonmechanized jobs and office machine operators who were above the median on the Self-Evaluative Involvement scale was not statistically significant. Computer operators had a higher percentage above the median than either traditional clerical employees or office machine operators. The percentage difference was significant at an acceptable level ($P < .05$) in the case of traditional nonmechanized clerks but not in the comparison with office machine operators ($P < .01$).

Self-evaluative involvement in work was slightly higher among systems analysts than among programmers (64 and 54 percent); the difference, however, was not statistically significant. Software personnel as a whole had a higher percentage above this scale median than did clerks performing traditional clerical duties (56 versus 46 percent; $P < .01$). In combination, office employees in software were not significantly different from office machine operators and computer operators.

Table 5.4 also contains the results of the test of this hypothesis for male and female subsamples. Significant differences between man-machine relationships did not appear among males or females when considered alone. It is worth noting, however, that among males per-

Table 5.4
Percentage above the Median on the Scale of Self-Evaluative Involvement in Work by Phases in the Man-Machine Relationship for the Total Sample, Males and Females

Self-Evaluative Involvement in Work Scale	Phases in the Man-Machine Relationship					
			Automated			
	Non-mechanized	Mechanized (EDP and Non-EDP)	(Computer Operators)	(Computer Software Personnel Combined)	Programmers	Systems Analysts
Total Sample above Median	46% (438)	49% (257)	57% (69)	56% (120)[a]	54% (95)	64% (25)
Males above Median	57 (37)	68 (45)	57 (68)	62 (87)[b]		
Females above Median	46 (401)	45 (212)	—[c]	45 (33)[d]		

[a] N. S.
[b] N. S.
[c] Since there were only two female computer operators, they have been excluded from this part of the analysis.
[d] N. S.

forming nonmechanized tasks 57 percent were above
the median on the Self-Evaluative Involvement scale,
a level equal to that of male computer operators. Moreover, 68 percent of the male machine operators were
above the median, 11 percent more than in the case
of computer operators.

Females tended to be less self-involved in work than
males in each man-machine relationship. A slightly
larger percentage of male clerks in nonmechanized jobs
are above the median on the Self-Evaluative Involvement scale than are females in nonmechanized jobs; the
difference is not significant. Similarly, 68 percent of
the male machine operators are above the median compared to 45 percent of the females in this man-machine
relationship $(P < .001)$. Finally, females in software jobs
are less self-involved in work than males in similar jobs
$(P < .05)$.

Mechanization in the office, whether in the form of
EDP or non-EDP-related operations, seemed to have a
similar effect on self-involvement in the work role. For
the total sample 50 percent of the non-EDP machine
operators were above the median on the Self-Evaluative
Involvement scale as were 47 percent of EDP-related
machine operators.[13]

A test of the association between the phases in the man-
machine relationship and the last alienation dimension,
instrumental work orientation, revealed a pattern much
like the one found with self-evaluative involvement
in work. Table 5.5 shows that office machine operators
hold no more of an instrumental view of their work
than the clerks in nonmechanized jobs. But office workers in both of these man-machine relationships are significantly higher on the Instrumental Work Orientation

---

13. These percentages are not contained in Table 5.4.

Table 5.5
Percentage above the Median on the Instrumental Work Orientation Scale by Phases in the Man-Machine Relationship for the Total Sample, Males and Females

| | Phases in the Man-Machine Relationship | | | | | |
| | | | Automated | | | |
Instrumental Work Orientation Scale	Non-mechanized	Mechanized (EDP and Non-EDP)	(Computer Operators)	(Computer Software Personnel Combined)	Programmers	Systems Analysts
Total Sample above Median	55% (516)	54% (283)	30% (36)	19% (41)[a]	21% (36)	13% (5)
Males above Median	44 (28)	40 (24)	29 (35)	21 (29)[b]		
Females above Median	55 (488)	57 (259)	—[c]	17 (12)[d]		

[a] $X^2 = 112.10$, $df = 4$, $P < .001$, $\overline{C} = .33$
[b] $X^2 = 12.82$, $df = 4$, $P < .02$, $\overline{C} = .25$
[c] Since there were only two female computer operators, they have been excluded from this part of the analysis.
[d] $X^2 = 40.86$, $df = 4$, $P < .001$, $\overline{C} = .23$

scale than were computer operators (55 and 54 percent compared to 30 percent; $P < .001$).

Programmers and systems analysts were quite similar in terms of the extent to which they viewed their work as a means of enabling them to engage in nonwork activities that they considered more meaningful than work; only 21 and 23 percent, in that order, were above the Instrumental Work Orientation scale median. Together, 19 percent of the software personnel were above the scale median, while 55 percent of the traditional clerks and 54 percent of the office machine operators were similarly classified (percentage differences in both instances were significant at the .001 level). A considerably smaller percentage spread existed between computer operators and software personnel; however, the difference between 30 and 19 percent was statistically significant $(P < .05)$.

When males and females are considered alone, the curvilinear pattern remains for both sexes. Though males in the nonmechanized man-machine relationship had a smaller percentage instrumentally oriented than did females (44 and 55 percent), the spread was not significant. A statistically reliable difference in the same direction does appear in the comparison of males and females in the mechanized man-machine relationship $(P < .01)$. Males and females in software jobs have about the same low percentage above the median (21 and 17 percent).

As in the case for each alienation dimension except normlessness, the type of mechanization (EDP versus non-EDP) was not associated with a marked percentage disparity. Fifty-seven percent and 52 percent of non-EDP machine operators and EDP-related machine operators, respectively, ranked above the median on the Instrumental Work Orientation scale.

ORGANIZATIONAL VARIATIONS IN ALIENATION
Many factors may affect the level of alienation in addition to the relationship to technology at work. Examination of one possible variable, sex, has shown that the same pattern of alienation exists among males and females. A host of influences on alienation exist in any given company, and unique features of an organization besides technological relationships could produce variations in the level of alienation. With this in mind, further tests of the hypotheses were made, this time examining the relationships between worker-technology arrangements and alienation by company. Due to the small size of the software personnel and computer operator samples in each small insurance company, these four companies were consolidated. Table 5.6 contains the results of the tests of the hypotheses for the total sample, the large insurance company, the small insurance companies combined, and the bank.

A brief statement on these results will involve two types of comparisons. First, the relationships between the phases in the man-machine relationship and each alienation dimension will be considered within each of the organizational categories. Second, workers in each man-machine relationship will be compared with those in the same man-machine relationship in all other organizations. Since the results of both of these types of comparisons are largely consistent with the findings for the total sample, only general statements are necessary.

Despite some variations, the figures in Table 5.6 permit the conclusion that a similar pattern of association between the phases in the man-machine relationship and alienation appears among respondents in the large insurance company, the small insurance companies, and the bank. These variations within companies are unsystematic, revealing no consistent pattern.

Table 5.6
Percentage above the Median on Each Alienation Dimension by Man-Machine Relationship for the Total Sample, the Large Insurance Company, the Small Insurance Companies Combined, and the Bank

Alienation Dimensions	Phases in the Man-Machine Relationship						Automated			
	Non-mechanized		Mechanized			(Computer Operators)		(Computer Software Personnel)	
Powerlessness										
Total Sample	53%	(464)	58%	(281)		61%	(73)	9%	(18)
Large Insurance Company	54	(311)	48	(82)		70	(33)	12	(10)
Small Insurance Companies Combined	46	(55)	63	(83)		67	(14)	8	(4)
Bank	53	(98)	63	(116)		51	(26)	6	(4)
Meaninglessness										
Total Sample	52	(496)	63	(329)		48	(59)	34	(73)
Large Insurance Company	54	(332)	65	(118)		39	(19)	38	(34)
Small Insurance Companies Combined	41	(53)	58	(83)		62	(13)	33	(17)
Bank	56	(111)	64	(128)		52	(27)	31	(22)
Normlessness										
Total Sample	49	(461)	49	(255)		34	(41)	37	(77)
Large Insurance Company	48	(293)	48	(86)		34	(17)	38	(33)
Small Insurance Companies Combined	55	(69)	54	(77)		38	(8)	47	(24)
Bank	50	(99)	47	(92)		31	(16)	29	(20)
Self-Evaluative Involvement										
Total Sample	46	(438)	49	(257)		57	(69)	56	(120)
Large Insurance Company	46	(287)	56	(100)		54	(26)	56	(50)
Small Insurance Companies Combined	51	(64)	45	(66)		62	(13)	59	(31)
Bank	44	(87)	45	(91)		58	(30)	56	(39)
Instrumental Work Orientation										
Total Sample	55	(516)	54	(283)		30	(36)	20	(41)
Large Insurance Company	55	(338)	48	(84)		33	(16)	14	(12)
Small Insurance Companies Combined	46	(57)	64	(93)		33	(7)	31	(16)
Bank	62	(121)	54	(106)		25	(13)	19	(13)

Examination of employees in each man-machine relationship by company substantiates this conclusion from a different but related perspective. Inspection of Table 5.6 will make it apparent that the level of alienation characteristic of employees in each man-machine relationship tended to remain constant from one organization to another. For example, on the Powerlessness scale 12 percent of the computer software personnel in the large insurance company were above the median as were 8 percent of the programmers and systems analysts in the bank and 6 percent of those in small insurance companies combined. Again, with some unsystematic variations, employees in each man-machine relationship in each company had nearly the same percentages (that is, the percentages were not significantly different) above the median on each alienation scale.

To sum up, examination of variations in the level of alienation among man-machine relationships within each company and between organizations did not turn up any consistent differences. The hypothesized effect of worker relationship to technology on alienation was sustained within and between organizations of different size and industry (banking and insurance).

SUMMARY
After the maze of detailed findings presented in this chapter a summary will be helpful. Further interpretation of the results is left for the final chapter.

It was predicted that the curvilinear relationship between the phases in the man-machine relationship and the alienation dimensions found among factory workers would also appear in the office. These expectations were largely supported, particularly among males.

No significant differences were found among more traditional clerks, office machine operators, and computer operators in terms of the degree of perceived freedom and control at work (powerlessness). In fact, lack of freedom and control on the job showed a tendency to increase as the level of technology advanced, up to and including computer operators. That is, workers in mechanized jobs had a somewhat higher percentage above the median on the Powerlessness scale than clerks holding nonmechanized jobs; and computer operators exhibited a slightly higher degree of powerlessness than did employees in mechanized jobs. However, computer software personnel displayed markedly less powerlessness than the other three types of office employees. Examination of this relationship among males and females separately revealed the same pattern for both sexes, though females tended to be slightly more alienated than males in the same relationship to technology.[14]

The predicted curvilinear relationship also held with respect to meaninglessness. Clerks in nonmechanized jobs, computer operators and programmers and systems analysts were significantly lower than office machine operators in terms of a perceived lack of connection between their jobs and the jobs of others. Dividing the males and females for a similar test revealed no change in the pattern of relationship, though females in computer software positions were more alienated than male programmers and systems analysts.

Workers in each of the relationships to technology at work were compared regarding the degree to which those in each felt that promotion in their companies was based on nonmerit criteria such as pull and connection. Normlessness was no more prevalent among machine-operating than among non-machine-operating

---

14. It will be remembered that because there were only two female computer operators they were excluded from the controlled tests of association for all alienation dimensions.

office personnel. However, computer operators and computer software personnel showed a significantly lower percentage above the median on this scale than workers in either of the other two man-machine relationships.

As for the total sample, male and female nonmachine operators were not significantly less normless than machine operators of each sex. Among males, however, office machine operators were significantly higher on normlessness than computer operators, while non-machine-operating males were not. Male computer software personnel were lower on normlessness than male traditional clerks and machine operators and had about the same percentage above the Normlessness scale median as computer operators. A curvilinear pattern was not evident among females. Female programmers and systems analysts were significantly higher on norm-lessness than their male counterparts; and, as a consequence, females in computer software jobs showed a level of alienation on the Normlessness scale commensurate with female clerks and machine operators.

Office employees in nonmechanized jobs were not more self-involved in work than machine operators. Non-mechanized clerks were significantly lower on the extent to which they judged themselves in terms of their work than computer operators and software personnel, but office machine operators, while having a smaller percentage above the median on the Self-Evaluative Involvement in work scale, were not significantly different from computer operators or computer software personnel. The pattern of relationship was not substantially altered when males and females were considered separately. Computer operators, software personnel, and male clerks in nonmechanized jobs displayed only slight percentage differences above the median. Male machine operators had a larger percentage above the median than either of the two man-machine relationships, but the percentage spread was not significant at the .05 level. Similarly, females in each man-machine relationship had almost identical percentages above the Self-Evaluative Involvement scale median. Females tended to be less ego-involved in their work than males in each man-machine relationship. For the machine-operating and computer software comparisons the differences were statistically significant.

On the last alienation dimension, instrumental work orientation, machine-operating and non-machine-operating office workers had nearly the same percentage above the scale median. Employees in both of these man-machine relationships had a significantly higher percentage who viewed work as a means to ends outside of work than did computer operators or programmers and systems analysts. When males were examined alone, percentage differences between traditional clerk, machine operators, and computer operators were not significant, but the pattern of relationship remained unchanged. Males in software jobs were significantly less instrumentally oriented than clerks or office machine operators. Females in the mechanized and nonmechanized machine relationships were not significantly different in terms of instrumentality, but female programmers and systems analysts were significantly less alienated than traditional clerks and office machine operators.

In the last section of this chapter the relationship between the phases in the man-machine relationship and the alienation dimensions were examined within the large insurance company, the bank, and the four small insurance companies combined. A similar trend in the level of alienation by man-machine relationship held in each organizational category. Comparisons of the level of alienation in each man-machine relationship across organizational settings revealed no consistent variations.

Chapter 6 contains a report of the comparative levels of alienation among manual and nonmanual workers, including some conclusions on the similarity between the nature of work and worker attitudes in the office and factory. A final chapter is devoted to an overview of the impact of mechanization and automation on alienation from work. A summary of the findings for office and factory workers separately opens this concluding chapter. Some implications of the study complete the volume.

6 Comparison of Office and Factory Workers

A theme in the automation literature is that factory and office work are becoming increasingly similar, diminishing manual-nonmanual differences in work and work attitudes. Even before the current interest in the impact of computers on white-collar employees came into vogue, Mills depicted office workers as the new proletariat.[1] Organizational expansion, centralization, specialization, and technology, the argument goes, conjoin to make the office much like the factory. A sense of craftsmanship is said to be lost, as freedom and control and a sense of interconnection among jobs disappear, and specialization and standardization ascend in the organization of labor in the office. Mills wrote that these changes could produce social-psychological separation from work among white-collar employees:

If they [office workers] do not learn from their work or develop themselves in doing it, in time, they cease trying to do so, often having no interest in self-development even in other areas. . . . If their way of earning a living does not infuse their mode of living, they try to build their real life outside their work. Work becomes a sacrifice of time, necessary to building a life outside of it.[2]

Since Mills, some researchers of office automation have observed a narrowing of the gap between white-collar and blue-collar work and conditions of employment.[3]

---

1. C. Wright Mills, *White-Collar* (New York: Oxford University Press, 1956), pp. 189–228.
2. *Ibid.,* p. 228.
3. Leonard Rico, *The Advance Against Paperwork* (Ann Arbor: Bureau of Industrial Relations, Graduate School of Business Administration, University of Michigan, 1967), pp. 215–231; Floyd C. Mann and Lawrence K. Williams, "Organizational Impact of White-Collar Automation," *Annual Proceedings,* Industrial Relations Research Association (December 1958), pp. 65–66; Ida

If Mills and others are correct, if the traditional gap between factory and office work situations is closing, then comparisons between office and factory workers should reveal little difference in alienation levels.

From the framework of the present study it follows that gross comparisons of blue-collar and white-collar workers is not as meaningful as comparisons between both types of workers in similar relationships to technology at work. Tests of the levels of alienation between white- and blue-collar workers will be primarily between workers standing in similar relationships to technology. Computer operators and computer software personnel will be compared with oil refinery monitors, automobile assemblers with office machine operators, and automobile factory craftsmen with nonmechanized clerical employees. In the process, each type of office worker will be compared with assemblers, since semiskilled factory workers best approximate the image Mills and others have in mind when they draw parallels between office and factory work.

Table 6.1 contains the percentage of both blue- and white-collar workers in each man-machine relationship above the median on each alienation scale. Considering first the nonmechanized man-machine relationship, it is apparent that craftsmen feel significantly less powerlessness than either male or female nonmechanized clerks (19 percent for craftsman versus 53 percent for female and 42 percent for male nonmechanized office workers). On the scales of Meaninglessness, Normlessness, Self-Evaluative Involvement, and Instrumental Work Orientation, only small percentage differences

---

R. Hoos, *Automation in the Office* (Washington, D.C.: Public Affairs Press, 1961), pp. 123ff; Enid Mumford and Olive Banks, *The Computer and the Clerk* (London: Routledge & Kegan Paul, 1967), pp. 183ff.

Table 6.1
Percentage of Blue- and White-Collar Workers above the Median on Each Alienation Scale by Phases in the Man-Machine Relationship

| | Phases in the Man-Machine Relationship | | | | |
| | Nonmechanized | | Mechanized | Automated | |
Alienation Scales	(Craftsmen)	(Traditional Clerical)		(Machine Monitors)	(Computer-Software Personnel)
Powerlessness					
Blue-Collar	19% (22)	—	94% (87)	42% (36)	—
White-Collar	—	53% (464)	58 (281)	61 (73)	9% (18)
Males	—	42 (26)	50 (31)	62 (73)	7 (9)
Females	—	53 (438)	59 (250)	—	12 (9)
Meaninglessness					
Blue-Collar	46 (52)	—	73 (68)	45 (38)	—
White-Collar	—	52 (496)	63 (329)	48 (59)	34 (73)
Males	—	44 (28)	65 (43)	48 (57)	30 (41)
Females	—	55 (468)	62 (286)	—	44 (32)

Normlessness	48 (54)				
Blue-Collar	—	49 (461)	61 (57)	33 (28)	—
White-Collar	—	45 (29)	49 (255)	34 (41)	37 (77)
Males	—	50 (432)	56 (36)	34 (40)	30 (42)
Females			52 (219)	—	52 (35)
Self-Evaluative Involvement	48 (56)				
Blue-Collar	—	46 (438)	38 (37)	70 (64)	—
White-Collar	—	57 (37)	49 (257)	57 (69)	56 (120)
Males	—	46 (401)	68 (45)	57 (68)	62 (87)
Females			45 (212)	—	45 (33)
Instrumental Work Orientation	50 (56)				
Blue-Collar	—	55 (516)	69 (64)	29 (25)	—
White-Collar	—	44 (28)	54 (283)	30 (36)	19 (41)
Males	—	55 (480)	40 (24)	29 (35)	21 (29)
Females			57 (259)	—	17 (12)

[a] The two female computer operators were excluded from separate analysis.

(all less than 10 percent) exist between craftsmen and male and female clerks; no differences were statistically significant.

Male office machine operators are less alienated than assemblers on the scales of Powerlessness (50 percent versus 94 percent), Self-Evaluative Involvement (68 percent versus 38 percent), and Instrumental Work Orientation (40 percent versus 69 percent). Though not statistically significant, the same trend appears on the normlessness and meaninglessness dimensions. Seventy-three percent of the assemblers are above the median on the Meaninglessness Scale compared to 65 percent of the male office machine operators; 56 percent of these office workers are high on normlessness, while 61 percent of the assemblers are above the median on this scale.

Comparing females in mechanized jobs to assemblers reveals the same trend. Female machine-operating office employees are less alienated than automobile assembly-line workers on each dimension. Only on the Self-Evaluative Involvement Scale was a difference (a spread of 7 percent) not significant.

With two exceptions (powerlessness and self-evaluative involvement), computer operators and oil refinery control room monitors show nearly the same percentages above each scale median. Among monitors a sense of powerlessness is significantly less prevalent than among computer operators (42 and 61 percent, respectively). Seventy percent of the monitors are above the median on self-evaluative involvement compared to 57 percent of the computer operators. On the other three alienation dimensions the percentage differences between monitors and computer operators range from only 1 to 3 percent.

A final comparison between office and factory workers in the same man-machine relationship involves oil refinery monitors and computer software personnel. Male programmers and systems analysts are less powerless than monitors (7 versus 42 percent above the scale median) and experienced meaninglessness to a significantly lower degree than monitors. On the other three dimensions of alienation no real differences appeared between monitors and males performing computer software functions.

When comparing female computer software personnel with monitors, a different pattern appeared. Like males, female programmers and systems analysts feel a lack of freedom and control at a level considerably below monitors (12 versus 42 percent above the scale median), and females in computer software jobs are less instrumentally oriented than oil refinery monitors (17 versus 29 percent). On the other hand, monitors are more self-involved in work and feel less normless than female programmers and systems analysts. With respect to meaninglessness a spread of only 1 percent separates workers in these two man-machine relationships.

SUMMARY AND CONCLUSIONS
A number of studies, conducted before factory and office automation captured the spotlight, compared work attitudes of manual and nonmanual workers. This literature suggested that workers in higher status (that is, white-collar) occupations are more likely to value the intrinsic aspects of their jobs than are workers in lower status (that is, blue-collar) occupations. For example, Jurgensen[4] found that blue-collar workers ranked job aspects in this order: security, advancement, type of work. Sales and clerical workers reversed this order, placing type of work first, advancement second, and

---

4. Clifford E. Jurgensen, "Selected Factors Which Influence Job Preference," *Journal of Applied Psychology*, 31 (December 1947), pp. 553–564.

security last. Economic rewards received a higher rank among the blue-collar than among the white-collar workers. In a similar study Lindahl [5] asked factory and office workers to compare ten job aspects. Office workers gave the highest average rank to interesting work. Security was accorded the highest average rank by factory workers. A nationwide study conducted by Centers [6] indicated that manual workers were less likely than business, professional, and other white-collar respondents to mention a feature of the work itself as a reason for liking their jobs. A larger proportion of manual workers mentioned economic rewards.

Internally undifferentiated comparisons of white- and blue-collar workers, as in the studies cited, show nonmanual employees to have a higher level of job satisfaction than manual workers. More detailed analyses reveal that skilled blue-collar workers and lower-level clerical employees have about the same levels of job satisfaction.[7]

---

5. Lawrence G. Lindahl, "What Makes a Good Job," *Personnel,* 25 (January 1949), pp. 263–266.
6. Richard Centers, "Motivational Aspects of Occupational Stratification," *Journal of Social Psychology,* 28 (November 1948), pp. 187–217. For additional studies see Elizabeth Lyman, "Occupational Differences in the Value Attached to Work," *American Journal of Sociology,* 61 (September 1955), pp. 138–144; Herbert H. Hyman, "The Value Systems of Different Classes: A Social-Psychological Contribution to the Analysis of Stratification," *Class, Status, and Power,* edited by Reinhard Bendix and Seymour Lipset (Glencoe, Illinois: The Free Press, 1953), pp. 426–442; Robert Dubin, "Industrial Workers' Worlds: A Study of the 'Central Life Interests' of Industrial Workers," *Social Problems,* 3 (January 1956), pp. 131–142; and Louis H. Orzack, "Work as a 'Central Life Interest' of Professionals," *Social Problems,* 7 (Fall 1959), pp. 125–132.
7. See Robert Blauner, "Work Satisfaction and Industrial Trends in Modern Society," in *Labor and Trade Unionism,* edited by Walter Galenson and Seymour Martin Lipset (New York: John

In the present study, office employees of both sexes
in more traditional clerical jobs exhibited about the
same levels of alienation as factory craftsmen except that
the latter felt that they have more freedom and control
in work than the former. Such a finding is not unfavorable for these office workers since they tended to be
no more alienated than a highly skilled type of factory
worker. It is particularly important that clerks in nonmechanized jobs were as self-involved in and intrinsically oriented toward their jobs as were craftsmen. There
is a convergence between factory and office workers in
these kinds of jobs, but it should not be interpreted as
being detrimental to office workers.

Office machine operators of both sexes were less alienated than assemblers on each scale, though a few of the
differences were not significantly different at the .05
level. This may be interpreted as additional evidence
that clerical workers, even in the case of machine-
operating personnel, are not losing ground in the sense
of holding attitudes similar to semiskilled factory
workers. This is also true for the other man-machine
relationships since office employees of both sexes in each
of the other man-machine relationships were either
quite similar to office machine operators in their levels
of alienation, as in the case of more traditional clerks,
or less alienated, as were computer software personnel
and computer operators.

An important finding emerged in the comparison
between monitors and computer operators. Monitors
in oil refining control rooms and computer operators
were almost identical on the meaninglessness, norm-

Wiley & Sons, Inc., 1960), p. 342; and Harold L. Wilensky, "Varieties of Work Experience," in *Man in a World of Work,* edited
by Henry Borow (Boston: Houghton Mifflin Company, 1964),
p. 137.

lessness, and instrumental work orientation dimensions of alienation. However, lack of freedom and control was significantly more prevalent among computer operators in the office than among monitors in the refinery (a difference of 20 percent); and 13 percent more of the monitors were self-involved in work than were computer operators. In sum, computer operators were either as high or higher on the alienation dimensions than factory workers in the automated man-machine relationship. Why? It cannot be said that computer operators have experienced downgrading. Computer operators are near the top of the clerical occupational structure; they have either been promoted from lower-level clerical jobs or have taken their positions as a first job in their companies. One could argue that computer operators are working under more factorylike conditions and are consequently similar in work attitudes to monitors.

There is an explanation for the convergence in work attitudes among monitors and computer operators that is consistent with the conclusion that mechanized and nonmechanized office workers are less alienated than semiskilled factory workers and on most scales no more alienated than skilled craftsmen: operators in continuous-process industries, such as oil refining, perform tasks and work under conditions much more similar to office employees than have any other factory workers before automation. A balanced, and probably correct, assessment is given by Wedderburn, who sees the impact of automation in the office and factory on job content this way:

All these trends suggest a narrowing of traditional differentiation in terms of job content. What have hitherto been manual jobs . . . have an increasing conceptual content, and an increasing emphasis upon formal knowledge. On the other hand some clerical jobs [presumably including computer operators] have an increasing manual content with the advent of computers.[8]

Three conclusions may be offered from this line of interpretation:

1. Contrary to a popular prediction, mechanization and computerization have not made office employees as alienated from work as semiskilled factory workers. Computer operators, office machine operators, traditional-type clerical workers, and software personnel are all less alienated than assembly-line workers, the prototypal factory worker.

Moreover, the following series of findings indicate that office employees in all man-machine relationships compare favorably with craftsmen: (a) Nonmechanized clerical employees, except for powerlessness, are not significantly more alienated than skilled craftsmen. (b) Office machine operators have less freedom and control on the job and lack a sense of job interconnection to a greater degree than do craftsmen. But clerical employees in mechanized jobs show a level of alienation no higher than craftsmen on the Normlessness, Self-Evaluative Involvement, and Instrumental Work Orientation scales. (c) Computer operators have less freedom and control than maintenance craftsmen, but they experience the same level of meaning and are less alienated than craftsmen on the Normlessness, Self-Evaluative Involvement, and Instrumental Work Orientation scales. (d) Software personnel are less alienated on each scale than skilled craftsmen.

---

8. Dorothy Wedderburn, "Are White-Collar and Blue-Collar Jobs Converging? The Impact of Technology Upon Occupational-Structure and Content" (Oberhausen, Germany: Document of the Third International Conference on Rationalization, Automation and Technological Change, sponsored by the Industrial Metalworkers' Industrial Union of the Federal Republic of Germany, 1968), p. 11.

2. It is true that traditional nonmechanized clerks and office machine operators tend to be more alienated than operators in a continuous-process plant. At the same time these two types of office workers also tend to be more alienated than computer operators. And some similarity in work attitudes appeared between monitors of an integrated production system and computer operators and computer software personnel. This leads to a second conclusion. Continuous-process technology in the factory may create a job situation, as reflected in levels of alienation, for operators that is closer to the office than the traditional factory.

3. The third conclusion is based on the first two. *A convergence in work attitudes may be occurring between office computer operators and continuous-process monitors but, according to these data, it cannot be said that mechanized and automated technology in the office has led to a convergence between blue- and white-collar workers as a whole.* Phrased in a way consistent with the broader framework of this study, any generalization concerning the convergence in work attitudes among blue- and white-collar workers must take into account variations in man-machine relationships within and between each occupational grouping.

7 Mechanization, Automation, and Alienation in the Factory and Office: An Overview

Underlying this study was the following question: Does a worker's unique relationship to technology engender in him a set of feelings about work that is distinguishable from others laboring under different man-machine relationships? To explore this question, three man-machine relationships were sampled in the office and factory. These man-machine relationships were workers in a nonmechanized production system, machine operators in a mechanized production system, and operators or monitors in an automated production system. Built into this independent variable were two important ideas. One is that each man-machine relationship is associated with a historical stage in the development of technology from premechanization to mechanization to automation in both offices and factories. A second important idea is that a different degree of functional specialization is associated with each phase in the man-machine relationship: nonmechanized—lower specialization, mechanized—higher specialization, and automated—lower specialization. Variations in alienation from work were examined through comparisons of samples of blue- and white-collar workers representing each of these three man-machine relationships.

SUMMARY OF THE FINDINGS

Factory Workers
Among factory workers curvilinear associations were found between the phases in the man-machine relationship and each of five alienation scales (Powerlessness, Meaninglessness, Normlessness, Self-Evaluative Involvement in work, and Instrumental Work Orienta-

tion). Alienation was lower among skilled maintenance workers in an automobile factory, reached a peak among final assemblers in the same auto factory, and declined again among monitors in an oil refinery, on all but the Powerlessness scale, to a point below that of either assemblers or craftsmen.

Somewhat surprising was the fact that, except for powerlessness, monitors displayed relatively less alienation than craftsmen. However, practicing a craft in a large bureaucratic organization may be quite different from the exercise of skill as a traditional, "independent" artisan. Further research should include a comparison of monitors in a continuous-process industry with independent craftsmen such as those in construction or craftsmen engaged in turning out handmade products. Of course, independent artisans are disappearing, much as independent soldiers, inventors, and scientists are doing.

Office Employees

On the white-collar side, samples to represent each man-machine relationship were obtained from a large insurance company, four small insurance companies, and a large bank. The nonmechanized man-machine relationship in the office was represented by office employees performing more traditional clerical duties (secretaries and clerks representing a variety of jobs and grade levels). The sample for the mechanized man-machine relationship contained office employees operating EDP-related machines (operators of keypunch, proof-encoding, and Flexowriting machines, and operators of other punched-card equipment such as sorters, tabulators, and reproducers) and non-EDP-related machine operators (typists, stenographers, MTST operators, clerk typists, Addressograph, and microfilm machine operators). Computer operators comprised one sample for the automated man-machine relationship in the office. A second sample fitting into the automated man-machine relationship was composed of computer software personnel (programmers and systems analysts).

Considering trends more than specific instances, the following patterns were observed among office employees:

1. Nonmechanized clerks exhibited the same levels of alienation as office machine operators.

2. EDP-related machine operators tended to be no more alienated than non-EDP-related office machine operators.

3. a. Except for powerlessness, computer operators tended to be less alienated than workers in either the nonmechanized or the mechanized man-machine relationship. Not all the differences, however, were statistically significant.

b. The level of powerlessness in work was nearly the same among office employees in nonmechanized, mechanized, and computer-operating jobs.

4. a. Programmers and systems analysts combined tended to be less alienated than employees in each of the other man-machine relationships, including computer operators.

b. Programmers and systems analysts tended to show the same levels of alienation; only on the Meaninglessness scale were programmers significantly more alienated than systems analysts.

5. a. There were no consistent differences between males and females in the nonmechanized and mechanized man-machine relationships on the Powerlessness, Meaninglessness, and Normlessness scales.

b. Males in the nonmechanized and mechanized man-machine relationships had a higher percentage above the median on the Self-Evaluative Involvement in work scale and a lower percentage above the Instrumental Work Orientation scale median than did females in these same relationships to technology. However, differences were statistically significant in only one comparison.

c. Females in computer software positions were no more powerlessness or instrumentally oriented than their male counterparts. But on the meaninglessness, normlessness, and self-evaluative involvement dimensions, female programmers and systems analysts were more alienated than males in the same jobs.

6. a. A very few unsystematic variations aside, the same pattern of alienation by man-machine relationship emerged within each organizational category (that is, the large insurance company, the large bank, and the four small insurance companies combined).

b. The levels of alienation among employees in each man-machine relationship were quite similar across each organizational category.

In summary, the curvilinear relationships between the phases in the man-machine relationship and alienation found among factory workers generally appeared among office employees. Software personnel and computer operators on nearly all alienation dimensions were lower than nonmechanized and mechanized clerical workers, the one exception being that computer operators were no less powerless than nonmechanized and mechanized office employees. Computer operators in this sample were manning second-generation computers. Third-generation computers along with other technological developments may eventually increase the amount of freedom and control in the computer operator's job. We will return to this point later when factory and office automation are distinguished as production systems.

Contrary to expectation, there was a fairly consistent

lack of difference between office machine operators and clerks in the traditional nonmechanized man-machine relationship. An important question is, why were the levels of alienation nearly the same for machine-operating and non-machine-operating office employees? One explanation consistent with the hypothesis that alienation increases with functional specialization is that, like office machine operators, clerks performing nonmechanized tasks have been subjected to job specialization. In the review of the literature on automation in the office in Chapter 4, it was observed that computerization results in the upgrading of non-machine-operating clerical jobs. An assumption made at that time was that an increase in job size was associated with upgrading. Can upgrading and increased job specialization among traditional nonmechanized clerical workers occur simultaneously? A satisfactory answer to this question cannot be provided from the data collected for this research. There is some evidence that suggests an affirmative answer to this question.

One explanation for the similar degree of alienation among clerks in nonmechanized and mechanized jobs is as follows.[1] Computers upgrade, or at a minimum, do not significantly downgrade clerical jobs. However, job grade level (which varies directly with salary) may be based not upon job size or skill but upon the requirement that employees do the precisely correct thing at the right time—that is, upon responsibility. As responsibility for accuracy and timing increase, so do job level

---

1. Whisler and Meyer offer this explanation by which upgrading and job specialization may well occur together among nonmechanized clerical employees affected by computerization. See Thomas L. Whisler and Harold Meyer, *The Impact of EDP on Life Company Organization* (Life Office Management Association, Personnel Administration Report, No. 34, 1967), p. 95.

and salary. Responsibility of this sort may be attached to minutely subdivided jobs or to jobs involving a variety of tasks.

It may be that the upgrading of non-machine-operating clerical workers as a result of computerization does not involve job enlargement but is a function of increased responsibility of the sort already described. Clerks may be subject to job size diminution that is not reflected in the job grade structure. From the data collected for this study it is not possible to determine the relative degree of functional specialization among nonmechanized clerical workers vis-à-vis office machine operators.[2]

A second, and related, explanation is that job specialization had already been occurring in the office prior to mechanization and computerization. The argument runs like this. As business volume has grown and as organizations have increased in size, the need for information processing and storage in offices created the

---

2. In a bank that had recently converted to computers, however, Mumford and Banks found that, while there were no cases of downgrading among clerks, both machine operators and control clerks had narrower functions and more routine jobs than before computerization. They also observed that among bank clerks interest and variety were the job aspects that decreased most after computerization, while accuracy and amount of work showed the greatest increase. See Enid Mumford and Olive Banks, *The Computer and the Clerk* (London: Routledge & Kegan Paul, 1967), pp. 185–190.

On the other hand, in study of clerks in a newly computerized insurance company, Hardin reported that while any changes in amount of work and accuracy required were primarily in the direction of an increase, an equal percentage of the office workers indicated increases in variety, responsibility, skill, and judgment in their jobs after computerization. See Einar Hardin, "The Reactions of Employees to Office Automation," *Monthly Labor Review*, 83 (September 1960), p. 928. In short, the evidence on this point is inconclusive.

necessity for an increasingly large and specialized clerical labor force. Office technology was applied to paperwork as another means of handling this meteoric expansion. Mechanization and computerization, then, have merely accelerated the pace at which clerical work is undergoing functional specialization.

An EDP executive in the large insurance company explained that computerization, conceived by management as a means of coping with their expanding information-handling needs, has not only met these needs but has contributed to further expansion. In so doing, computers have encouraged functional specialization. Growth in business volume and organization size, in which computers play an important role, have made it more efficient to move toward specialization and centralization.[3] For example, at one time in this company an individual might have had enough knowledge of the total operation of an organizational unit to give all the specifications needed by the software division for designing and programming a job. By contrast, in an advanced computer system a person may be responsible for only one particular phase or segment of the total unit's operation. Currently, in some units programmers and systems analysts must confer with several people in order to secure all specifications. An inference is that a similar trend toward job specialization may be occurring in the ranks of non-machine-operating clerks.

Finally, some would argue that clerks in nonmechanized jobs in computerized offices are alienated not just because of job specialization but because of other "factorylike" conditions under which clerks work.

---

3. For more on this point see "Mechanisation and Automation in Offices: III," *International Labour Review*, 81 (April 1960), p. 266, and Leonard Rico, *The Advance Against Paperwork* (Ann Arbor: Bureau of Industrial Relations Graduate School of Business Administration, University of Michigan, 1967), pp. 217–222.

Time pressures created by stiff deadlines, increases in the amount of work, increased requirements for accuracy, easy detection of errors, large offices, and centralization of functions, each contributes to the analogy between the factory and office.

Convergence in Levels of Alienation among Factory and Office Workers

Recent technological changes in the office and factory have led some to argue that office and factory workers are becoming similar in job situations and work attitudes. It is the image of the assembly-line worker that some who envision such a merger often evoke. To the contrary, both male and female office machine operators in the present study were consistently less alienated than the sample of automobile assembly-line workers. The differences were even more pronounced when assemblers were compared with nonmechanized clerks, computer operators and programmers, and systems analysts. In addition, surveys have indicated that skilled blue-collar workers have more positive attitudes toward work than lower-level clerical workers, but the results in the present study show that on most dimensions office machine operators and clerks in nonmechanized jobs were not significantly more alienated than craftsmen in the automobile factory. Particularly important is the fact that office machine operators and nonmechanized clerks were self-involved in work and noninstrumentally oriented toward work at almost the same levels as these craftsmen.[4]

It is also important that computer operators, who are

---

4. Of course, one has to keep in mind that these craftsmen were employed in a large factory, a factor that may have inflated their levels of alienation compared with independent skilled workers or craftsmen in small organizations or shops.

in the upper reaches of the nonsupervisory job grade
structure in the office, exhibited the same level of
meaning in work as craftsmen and were less alienated
than these skilled automobile workers in terms of
normlessness, self-evaluative involvement, and instrumental work orientation. Craftsmen were less powerless
than these second-generation computer operators, a
situation that may be altered with the introduction of
third-generation computers in the office. Elaboration
of this point will be made in the implications section of
this chapter. And computer software personnel, the
highest job grade levels created by computer technology,
were less alienated than these craftsmen on each
dimension.

Some convergence in alienation levels appeared between oil refinery monitors and computer operators and
computer software personnel, with a major variation
between computer operators and employees in software
jobs. Where differences did appear, computer operators,
all of whom were male, were more alienated than
monitors; this was the case on the powerlessness and
self-evaluative involvement dimensions. By contrast,
in instances where monitors and computer software
personnel were significantly different (powerlessness and
meaninglessness dimensions), male programmers and
systems analysts were less alienated than monitors. For
females in computer software jobs and monitors, the
pattern was mixed.

These data bearing on the levels of alienation among
factory and office workers make the following conclusions reasonable. First, technology in the office has not
led to a convergence in work attitudes among mass-
production factory workers and office employees in
any one of the man-machine relationships in the office.
Second, the convergence between craftsmen and nonmechanized and machine-operating clerks is not por-

tentous for office employees since research indicates that highly skilled blue-collar workers have more positive attitudes toward work than lower-level clerical personnel. Third, there is some convergence in attitudes among oil refinery monitors and computer operators and computer software personnel. It is likely that automated technology in the office and factory creates some commonality among workers most closely related to the technology.[5]

As stated in Chapter 6, a conclusion that mechanization and automation in the office has produced a convergence between office and factory workers as a whole does not appear warranted. Within both the blue- and white-collar ranks and in making comparisons between factory and office workers, account must be taken of variations by man-machine relationship.

IMPLICATIONS

Practical Implications

The findings have two practical implications. First, that alienation among craftsmen and monitors whose jobs are not highly specialized was lower than among automobile workers in highly specialized jobs lends further support to the use of job enlargement as a means for decreasing alienation among factory workers. Similarly, in the office, computer operators and software personnel

---

5. Broom and Selznick put it this way: "Automation may reduce the distinction between factory and office, between hand and brain work, which has been a central element in the stratification system of industrial society. Blue-collar operators in the new clean, office-like factories will be responsible employees, much like the white-collar employees in the new, more mechanized, factory-like offices." Leonard Broom and Philip Selznick, *Sociology*, fourth edition (New York: Harper and Row Publishers, Inc., 1968), p. 486.

were generally less alienated than office machine operators and nonmechanized clerks. The reduction of job
specialization, in this case through the creation of
new man-machine relationships in the office and factory,
appears to exercise salutary effects on work attitudes.
This conclusion fits well with other research in the
factory and office, which also points to the favorable
effect of job enlargement on work attitudes.[6]

Second, the thesis that automation reverses the historical trend toward increased alienation from work among
factory workers appears to be supported. Continuous-
process technology may provide factory workers with
jobs characterized by more freedom, control, meaning,
and self-involvement than some, extrapolating from the
experience of mass-production mechanization, have
predicted.

Some qualifications must accompany statements on
the second implication for office employees. Computer
operators do not have as much freedom and control
on the job as do monitors in a continuous-process factory. Neither do they possess any more freedom and
control in their work than do traditional nonmechanized clerks and office machine operators. The idea will
be elaborated shortly that third-generation computers
and other technological developments may increase
the amount of freedom and control among computer
operators in automated offices of the near future.

Compared to mechanized office workers, computer
operators possess a greater knowledge of the relationship of their jobs to the work of others and believe to a
greater extent that mobility in their companies is based
on merit and ability. Computer operators are also more
self-involved in their work and view their jobs less
instrumentally than do office machine operators. No

6. See Chapter 1, pp. 2–3.

difference appeared between computer operators and traditional clerks on the Meaninglessness scale, but the former are less alienated than the latter on all other dimensions. Software personnel, the other high-level occupational category created by office automation, are less alienated on all dimensions than nonmechanized and mechanized office employees.

In short, office automation creates some high-level jobs whose occupants are less alienated than other types of office workers. Herein lies a significant difference between factory and office automation. Continuous-process technology in the factory decreases alienation among the bulk of the labor force required to operate and maintain the production system. This is because automation in the factory tends to create a labor force largely composed of two types of workers, maintenance personnel and control room operators, both of whom have skilled and responsible jobs. Office automation, by contrast, raises the skill and responsibility level among software personnel and computer operators but concomitantly contributes to job specialization due to its need for special-purpose machine operators for data preparation. Whether office automation promotes specialization among nonmechanized clerks performing tasks geared to the computer system seems to be a moot question. At the present stage of technological development, nonmechanized clerks and special-purpose machine operators comprise the bulk of the clerical labor force. To the extent that computer technology promotes specialization among these types of office workers, it contributes to the maintenance of a labor force that will experience more rather than less alienation.

Increased specialization in more traditional clerical jobs, of course, cannot be attributed to computerization alone. Offices require a host of clerks to perform tasks unrelated to the computer system. All this raises the

question of whether computerization in the office at
its present level of development is not a form of automation different from that found in continuous-process
industries.

In Appendix B integration of the production process
and automatic control of a feedback nature are isolated
as two essential characteristics of an automated system.
The position is taken that automation is best viewed in
an evolutionary perspective. Materials-handling and
control components of technology may be either rudimentary or very well developed. Development of these
components of technology is a matter of degree. Computers in the office do not have the capacity for control
of a feedback nature. As one EDP manager put it,
"Computer operators are human warning lights."
Computer operators must correct an error or call on
someone else to correct it. The computer itself does not
have a self-correcting capacity; it does what it is told
very well, but only what it is told and then only when
its instructions are accurate.

More important in the present context, a computer
system in the office entails a certain level of development
in automatic materials handling, but the need for extensive data preparation by a multitude of employees
outside the computer room means that integration is
not as well developed as in a continuous-process production system in the factory. In Bright's[7] terms, computer technology in an office neither performs the
total sequence of events in the processing of data nor
handles all of the secondary activities in the firm's
production process. At the present time computerization
in the office does not produce a completely integrated

7. James R. Bright, *Automation and Management* (Boston: Division of Research, Graduate School of Business Administration,
Harvard University, 1958), pp. 39–41.

system of data processing comparable to the processing of chemicals or petroleum or the generation of electrical power. Until computer technology is sophisticated enough to eliminate preparatory machine operations and the need for a clerical labor force to perform preliminary steps in the processing of data and to handle secondary activities, it should not be equated with continuous-process automation in the factory.

Is computer technology evolving in the direction of a more fully integrated data-processing system? An affirmative reply requires evidence of a trend toward consolidation of information into master files in computerized companies with concomitant reductions in the employment of supportive machine-operating and clerical personnel. An extensive study by the Bureau of Labor Statistics involving 305 insurance companies clearly indicates that these trends are occurring in computerized companies.[8]

Precisely the same trends reported in this BLS study are occurring among supporting machine-operating positions in the bank and insurance companies in the present study. The number of persons in specific occupations were obtained from EDP executives for three periods: just prior to the installation of their first computer, just before the installation of their first computer in the IBM 360 series, and currently. In each company the number of electric accounting machine operators was declining, while the number of computer operators, programmers, and systems analysts was increasing. The number of key-punch operators in each company was declining in the large insurance company

---

8. U.S. Department of Labor, Bureau of Labor Statistics Bulletin Number 1468, *Impact of Office Automation in the Insurance Industry* (Washington, D.C.: U.S. Government Printing Office, 1966), pp. 34–43.

and remaining relatively constant in the other organizations. EDP managers were also asked what effect advances in computer technology in the future would have on these occupations in their industries in general. Further declines among employees in punch-card machine-operating jobs were predicted.

Insurance office employment is also heavily affected by the trend toward consolidation of formerly disparate records into a few master policy files. Prior to consolidation, various units were in charge of a segment of the total policy files. Separate files were kept for billing, claims, agents commissions, and so forth. The consolidation of records and operations into the computer system eliminates the necessity for separate departments. Programmed functions are processed and reconciled inside the computer.[9]

The greater the consolidation of company records into one or more master files from which the computer can be programmed to secure appropriate information that is achieved, the more valid the analogy between office automation and continuous-process technology. Even with consolidation, however, computer operators must mount tapes before each job is processed. Tape mounting and dismounting detracts from the analogy between factory and office automation because the sense of continuous flow is broken at frequent intervals. However, computer technology is developing in a direction that contributes to making automation in the office and factory more comparable.

Second-generation computers run one job at a time.

9. Master files are contained in storage either on tapes, disc drives, or in data cells. With random-access capability, any information on a policy can be secured by the computer almost instantaneously. The data transmission system at the large insurance company gives a response to a query in a few seconds. Strides toward even more rapid data transmission have already been made.

Time-sharing or multiprocessing is the prime differentiating characteristic of third-generation computers. Multiprocessing involves entry of several programs at a time into the computer. This does not mean that a third-generation computer performs operations on a number of programs at exactly the same time. If this were the case, the operator of a third-generation computer would be doing much the same job as a second-generation computer operator. At certain junctures in the processing of a job, a computer must stop manipulations on the data relevant to a particular program in order to retrieve information from storage. During this interim the third-generation computer, rather than standing idle as do second-generation models, begins manipulations on another program. When the information on the first program that was called from storage arrives, the third-generation computer will discontinue manipulation on the second job and return to the first one. This alternating pattern is repeated among several programs until all are completed. If it were possible to enter automatically into a third-generation computer all the programs needed for a computer-operating shift, and if the files were completely consolidated, the situation would be much like an automated oil refinery in which crude oil is introduced for continuous, uninterrupted processing.

Further research in organizations with third-generation computer systems and highly integrated information files should be conducted. One hypothesis is that powerlessness in particular, and alienation in general, will be lower among computer operators in such a system. Such research is hampered at this point in time by the scarcity of computer systems that could be called automated as the term has been developed here, but appropriate research settings will exist in the very near future. In fact, in the large insurance company, the bank, and

one small insurance company some multiprocessing is
currently operational, and one small insurance company
has plans for 1969–1970. Each of these companies has
advanced far along the path to consolidated master files.

THE IMPORTANCE OF MAN-MACHINE RELATIONSHIPS
A central argument advanced by Blauner is that industries vary by the nature of their technological production systems; each industry possesses a characteristic
form of production technology. On this basis, Blauner
proposes a subfield of industrial sociology to be called
the "sociology of industries." [10] The idea is to place
emphasis on the importance of individual industries
and groups of similar industries as units of economic
and social organization. In this way a systematic, comparative approach can supplant the previously held
notion of the industrial work environment as an undifferentiated mass.
    Internally, however, a factory most likely applies
different types of technology to various aspects of the
production process. This raises the question of internal
technological differences by industry and even by firm.
Blauner recognizes that complete homogeneity in any
given industry or firm is seldom the case. In acknowl-
edging a weakness in the "sociology of industries" perspective, Blauner makes a point very cogent for the
present study:
Just as industrial sociology fosters an undifferentiated view
of industry in general and tends to ignore differences among
industries, the "sociology of industries" exaggerates the
unity of an individual industry and necessarily underplays
the important variations within that industry, as well as
its similarities to other industries. Our understanding of
the conditions and causes of alienation in manual work

10. Robert Blauner, *Alienation and Freedom* (Chicago: University of Chicago Press, 1964).

would also be furthered by an intensive investigation which focused on the variations in worker freedoms and job attitudes among the firms within any one of the four industries I have considered.[11]

If man's relationship to technology at work contributes to the prediction of his work attitudes, then it is important not to combine different man-machine relationships into one category as one might do when making inter-industry comparisons. For example, a sample of automobile workers could conceivably contain craftsmen, assemblers, laborers, and janitors, each with a different relationship to technology.

The present study focused on man-machine relationships rather than industries. Factory and office workers in each of the three man-machine relationships were part of a larger work organization containing workers with relationships to technology quite different from their own. Large differences in alienation were manifested consistently between craftsmen and assemblers, though they were in the same industry, company, and local union. Consistent differences in alienation between office employees in each man-machine relationship appeared within each company; and levels of alienation among office workers in each man-machine relationship were comparable from one organization to another. Thus stronger credence is given to the impact of technology and job content upon work attitudes. More research is needed comparing workers within industries and firms laboring under different man-machine relationships.

Studying alienation at the industry level can have concrete implications for workers. The advent and development of the factory system of production has created a large body of semiskilled workers standing in

---

11. *Ibid.*, p. 187.

nearly the same relationship to technology at work. Automation in the factory also appears to have a somewhat uniform impact on the nature of work. On the other hand, computerization in the office has thus far resulted in the existence of markedly different worker relationships to technology even within a single organization. In addition, though valid data are hard to obtain and even more difficult to agree upon, it can be argued that automation has not enjoyed the widespread application predicted for it.[12] At least for a long period, the situation is likely to remain one of diversity in worker-technology relationships within industries and within companies.

WORK AND LEISURE

Another implication relates to the question of meaning in work versus meaning in leisure. Some observers have suggested that work is no longer an important arena for intrinsic satisfactions and feelings of personal worth. Dubin,[13] for example, concluded that for the majority of industrial workers nonwork activity has eclipsed work as a central life focus. There may have been an over-representation of functionally specialized workers in Dubin's sample; or if skilled workers had been excluded,

---

12. For a balanced position see William A. Faunce, *Problems of an Industrial Society* (New York: McGraw-Hill Book Company, 1968), pp. 51–61. Faunce concludes that industries which have not been affected by automation employ over half of the employed civilian labor force. Still, he estimates that in 1964, 17.2 percent (12.1 million workers) were employed in industries that were already automated, partially automated, or moving along that path. And federal, state, and local government employees were excluded from these figures, many of whom work in computerized offices.
13. Robert Dubin, "Industrial Workers' Worlds: A Study of the 'Central Life Interests' of Industrial Workers," *Social Problems,* 3 (January 1956), pp. 131–142.

the percentage abandoning work as a central life interest might have been greater. An important implication of the present study is that proportions of workers regarding work as a central life interest are likely to vary by man-machine relationship. Application of Dubin's "Central Life Interest" schedule in a study with a comparative design such as the one employed in the present research would be informative.

Pursuit of self-fulfilling experiences during nonworking hours may not be the sole alternative. Changes in man's relationship to technology at work may retain or resuscitate work as an integral part of life for many industrial workers and office employees. Assuming the validity of the findings reported in this monograph, a man-machine relationship favorable to work role attachment is created by continuous-process and computer automation. Enlargement of mechanized and nonmechanized jobs that are not or cannot be automated is crucial since the bulk of the labor force is employed in industries not yet affected by automation.

A CAVEAT ON TECHNOLOGY AND WORK ATTITUDES
Factors affecting attitudes toward work are too many, and their interrelationships too complex, to assume that the technologically determined attributes of the job alone constitute an explanatory variable. Blauner[14] concludes that differences in job satisfaction can be attributed to four factors: occupational prestige, control of work, work group integration, and the degree to which an "occupational community" exists among workers

---

14. Robert Blauner, "Work Satisfaction and Industrial Trends in Modern Society," in *Labor and Trade Unionism,* Walter Galenson and Seymour Martin Lipset (eds.) (New York: John Wiley & Sons, Inc., 1960), pp. 339–360.

while off the job. From a more extensive review of job satisfaction literature, Herzberg[15] and his associates ranked job factors affecting attitudes toward work in this order: security, opportunity for advancement, company and management, wages, intrinsic aspects of the job, supervision, social aspects of the job, communication, and working conditions. Intrinsic job content is correlated with many of the other factors, making it difficult to ascertain its contribution to the determination of attitudes toward work vis-à-vis the other variables. More recently, Turner and Lawrence[16] proposed a schema in which a number of variables intervene between technologically determined characteristics of work and such dependent variables as attendance, job satisfaction, and psychosomatic response. These "supplementary" variables include situational factors such as satisfaction with the company, supervision, work group, union, and pay, individual characteristics like age and education, and cultural differences as reflected in ethnic, religious, and rural-urban subcultures.

Walker and Guest take the extreme position that research on work attitudes that focuses solely on immediate job content is of slight value. There is little doubt that the "total job situation," including interpersonal relations on the job, pay, security, supervision, working conditions, promotion, and union, is necessary to account fully for all the variation in attitudes toward work. Nevertheless, the central purpose of the present investigation was to compare distinct worker relationships to

15. Frederick Herzberg, et al., Job Attitudes: Review of Research and Opinion (Pittsburgh: Psychological Service of Pittsburgh, 1957), pp. 72–79.
16. Arthur N. Turner and Paul R. Lawrence, Industrial Jobs and the Worker (Boston: Division of Research, Graduate School of Business Administration, Harvard University, 1965).

technology as they affect alienation from work. The impact of functional specialization on work attitudes is one often neglected by management and sometimes minimized by social scientists.

Appendix A Scale Construction

Scales of Powerlessness, Meaninglessness, Normlessness, Self-Evaluative Involvement in work, and Instrumental Work Orientation were formed separately for the blue- and white-collar samples.[1] Data collection among factory workers was accomplished with an interview schedule. As noted earlier, a much abbreviated form of this original research instrument had to be used in the case of clerical employees. In the paring process, some items originally included in the alienation scales for blue-collar workers were eliminated from the white-collar questionnaire. For comparability, identical items comprise each scale of alienation for both blue- and white-collar samples.

PROCEDURE

The following procedure was used in scale construction. A series of items included in the research instruments was formulated on the basis of concept definitions. The initial criterion for item inclusion was face validity. Each potential item for each scale was checked to make sure that the frequency of responses was adequately distributed along a continuum. Preponderant overloading of responses into one end of the continuum robs the item of power to differentiate subjects.

Each item showing an adequate frequency distribution along the continuum of responses for any particular scale was correlated with the sum of the scores of all the other items potentially to be included in the scale. Any standard regarding the value of a correlation coefficient

---

1. The original alienation scales for factory workers are contained in Jon M. Shepard, *Man-Machine Relationships, Attitudes Toward Work and Meanings in the Work Role.* Unpublished Doctoral Dissertation, Michigan State University, 1968, pp. 119–128.

sufficient for the inclusion of an item in a scale is arbitrary. With two exceptions, only items that showed correlations with the sum of the other items of .30 or above were retained. Information on the internal consistency of a scale is provided by the interitem correlations.

Items measuring powerlessness, meaninglessness, and normlessness each contained a characteristic of work. For each characteristic, respondents were to answer to what extent it existed in their job. Responses ranged from 1 ("minimum") to 7 ("maximum").[2] Scores on each item in each scale were merely summed. For example, for both blue- and white-collar samples eight items form the Powerlessness scale. Possible scores ranged from 8 (for persons answering "minimum" to all eight powerlessness items) to 56 (for persons responding "maximum" to all eight items).

For the blue-collar sample Self-Evaluative Involvement and Instrumental Work Orientation scales were formed by statements that could be answered by choosing one of five responses (that is, strongly agree, agree, undecided, disagree, strongly disagree). Each of these responses was assigned a numerical value from 1 ("low") to 5 ("high"). To illustrate, the Instrumental Work Orientation scale for blue-collar workers contained four items so that possible scores went from 4 to 20. The same items were used to construct scales of Self-Evaluative Involvement and Instrumental Work Orientation for the white-collar sample. However, the possible responses were expanded to include six responses: strongly agree; agree; undecided, lean toward

---

2. This technique is found in Lyman W. Porter, "A Study of Perceived Need Satisfaction in Bottom and Middle Management Jobs," *Journal of Applied Psychology,* 45 (February 1961), pp. 1–10.

agreement; undecided, lean toward disagreement; disagree; strongly disagree. For chi-square analysis, scale "scores" of 0 and 1 were assigned, broken as near the median as possible of each scale score distribution.

Powerlessness in Work

The items composing the Powerlessness scale refer to feelings of freedom and control on the job. Table A.1 contains the interitem correlations and correlations of single items to the sum of all other items for both the blue-collar and white-collar samples. Looking at the blue-collar sample first, the item-total correlations are all substantial (ranging from .46 to .63). All interitem correlations are near .40 except for those involving item 4. Even in the case of item 4 only one correlation falls below. 25 (correlation with item 6).

Item-total and interitem correlations for the white-collar sample are lower than for blue-collar workers. Nevertheless, item-total correlations, ranging as they did from .40 to .59, suggest that the items tap a common dimension for white-collar employees.

Meaninglessness in Work

This scale is concerned with the perceived connection of one's work to the jobs of others and to the larger organization. The correlations of single items with the sum of all other items are .50 or above for both the blue-collar and white-collar samples (Table A.2). Interitem correlations range from .48 to .57 for clerical personnel and from .45 to .58 for the factory workers.

NORMLESSNESS IN WORK

Normlessness questions were designed to measure the extent to which persons perceived mobility in their company to be based on nonmerit criteria. Correlations of single items to the sum of other items went from .46

Table A.1
Interitem Correlations and Item-Total Correlations:[a] Scale of Powerlessness in Work

	Interitem Correlations								Item-Total Correlations
	1	2	3	4	5	6	7	8	
1. To what extent can you vary the steps involved in doing your job?	1.00[b] (1.00)								.59 (.43)
2. To what extent can you move from your immediate working area during work hours?	.46 (.30)	1.00 (1.00)							.61 (.46)
3. To what extent can you control how much work you produce?	.38 (.29)	.46 (.20)	1.00 (1.00)						.58 (.47)
4. To what extent can you help decide on methods and procedures used in your job?	.39 (.38)	.26 (.31)	.38 (.38)	1.00 (1.00)					.45 (.56)
5. To what extent do you have influence over the things that happen to you at work?	.39 (.24)	.43 (.28)	.41 (.33)	.43 (.47)	1.00 (1.00)				.63 (.51)
6. To what extent can you do your work ahead and take a short rest break during work hours?	.38 (.25)	.48 (.34)	.35 (.29)	.20 (.31)	.42 (.33)	1.00 (1.00)			.54 (.48)
7. To what extent are you free from close supervision while doing your job?	.42 (.21)	.41 (.36)	.37 (.19)	.40 (.31)	.53 (.33)	.38 (.26)	1.00 (1.00)		.58 (.42)
8. To what extent can you increase the speed at which you do your work?	.49 (.19)	.45 (.19)	.50 (.37)	.26 (.24)	.44 (.25)	.46 (.33)	.36 (.18)	1.00 (1.00)	.62 (.40)

[a] Correlations for the blue-collar sample are based on $N = 302$. Correlations for the white-collar sample are based on $N = 1706$. Any correlation of .15 or above is significant at the .01 level for blue-collar workers. Considering white-collar employees a correlation as high as .08 is significant at the .01 level for a sample size of 1,000. Those in parentheses pertain to blue-collar workers. Those in parentheses refer to white-collar employees.
[b] Correlations not enclosed in parentheses pertain to blue-collar workers. Those in parentheses refer to white-collar employees.

Table A.2
Interitem Correlations and Item-Total Correlations:[a] Scale of
Meaninglessness in Work

	Interitem Correlations			Item-Total Correlations
	1	2	3	
1. To what extent do you know how your job fits into the total plant (operations of the company)?	1.00[b] (1.00)			.59 (.60)
2. To what extent do you know how your job fits in with the work of other departments in the plant (company)?	.58 (.57)	1.00 (1.00)		.66 (.64)
3. To what extent do you know how your work relates to the work of others that you work with?	.45 (.48)	.54 (.52)	1.00 (1.00)	.56 (.56)

[a] Correlations for the blue-collar sample are based on $N = 303$. Correlations for the white-collar sample are based on $N = 1821$. Any correlation of .15 or above is significant at the .01 level for blue-collar workers. Considering white-collar employees, a correlation as high as .08 is significant at the .01 level for a sample size of 1,000.
[b] Correlations not enclosed in parentheses pertain to blue-collar workers. Those in parentheses refer to white-collar employees.

to .58 among blue-collar workers and from .40 to .49
among clerical employees (Table A.3). Interitem correlations did not fall below .34 for either sample and
reached as high as .53.

SELF-EVALUATIVE INVOLVEMENT IN THE WORK ROLE
A scale of Self-Evaluative Involvement was constructed
to indicate the extent to which the worker feels that his
role is a more important referent for evaluating self than
activity in nonwork spheres. These two items were used
to measure this variable: "Success in the things you
do away from the job is more important to your opinion
of yourself than success in your work (occupational)
career" and "To you, your work (occupation) is only
a small part of who you are." They were significantly
correlated for both blue-collar ($r = .40$ based on $N =$

305) and white-collar employees ($r = .51$ based on $N = 1804$).

Instrumental Work Orientation is a measure of the extent to which work is considered to be primarily a means to ends outside of work as opposed to experiencing work activity as intrinsically meaningful. Table A.4 contains the correlations of single items to the sum

Table A.3
Interitem Correlations and Item-Total Correlations:[a] Scale of Normlessness in Work

Items	Interitem Correlations			Item-Total Correlations
	1	2	3	
1. To what extent do you feel that people who get ahead in the plant (company) deserve it?	1.00[b] (1.00)			.58 (.48)
2. To what extent do you feel that it is pull and connection that gets a person ahead in the plant (company)?	.44 (.34)	1.00 (1.00)		.46 (.40)
3. To what extent is getting ahead in the plant (company) based on ability?	.53 (.46)	.37 (.35)	1.00 (1.00)	.53 (.49)

[a] Correlations for the blue-collar sample are based on $N = 304$. Correlations for the white-collar sample are based on $N = 1800$. Any correlation of .15 or above is significant at the .01 level for blue-collar workers. Considering white-collar employees, a correlation as high as .08 is significant at the .01 level for a sample size of 1,000.
[b] Correlations not enclosed in parentheses pertain to blue-collar workers. Those in parentheses refer to white-collar employees.

of other items, which range from .37 to .48 among blue-collar workers and from .38 to .58 among the white-collar sample. The interitem correlations for both samples fell below .30 only in the case of items 1 and 4 ($r = .22$ and $r = .23$).

Table A.4

Interitem Correlations and Item-Total Correlations:[a] Scale of
Instrumental Work Orientation

	Interitem Correlations				Item-Total Correlations
	1	2	3	4	
1. Your job is something you have to do to earn a living; most of your real interests are centered outside your job (occupation).	1.00[b] (1.00)				.38 (.38)
2. Money is the most rewarding reason for working.	.32 (.31)	1.00 (1.00)			.44 (.54)
3. Working is a necessary evil to provide things your family and you want.	.31 (.36)	.38 (.54)	1.00 (1.00)		.48 (.58)
4. You are living for the day when you can collect your retirement and do the things that are important to you.	.22 (.23)	.27 (.34)	.34 (.36)	1.00 (1.00)	.37 (.41)

[a] Correlations for the blue-collar sample are based on $N = 304$. Correlations for the white-collar sample are based on $N = 1804$. Any correlation of .15 or above is significant at the .01 level for blue-collar workers. Considering white-collar employees a correlation as high as .08 is significant at the .01 level for a sample size of 1,000.
[b] Correlations not enclosed in parentheses pertain to blue-collar workers. Those in parentheses refer to white-collar employees.

Appendix B Distinction between Mechanization and Automation

Whatever the shortcomings of the literature on automation, a lack of definitions cannot be numbered among them. One point of contention underlying the various conceptions resides in whether one believes automation to be a novel technology or to be a continuation of the evolutionary advance of mechanization. The debate is crystalized in the works of Bright[1] and Diebold.[2] Taking an evolutionary point of view, Bright conceives of automation in the dictionary sense. That is, automation refers to making something more automatic than it has previously been. In Bright's mind "automaticity" involves an increase in control of operations by the technology itself and greater integration of the total production system.

The linking of control with automaticity can be seen in Bright's mechanization profile.[3] At the lowest level of mechanization involving handwork, hand tools, and power hand tools, man initiates control and the machine responds according to the worker's actions. The highest levels of mechanization include machines that can correct performance after operating, correct performance while operating, and anticipate required action and make adjustments. This level of mechanization

---

1. James R. Bright, *Automation and Management* (Boston: Division of Research, Graduate School of Business Administration, Harvard University, 1958), and "Does Automation Raise Skill Requirements?" *Harvard Business Review*, 36 (July–August 1958), pp. 85–98.
2. John Diebold, *Automation: The Advent of the Automatic Factory* (New York: D. Van Nostrand Co., Inc., 1952).
3. For the seventeen levels of mechanization and their relationship to power and control sources, see Bright, *Automation and Management,* p. 45.

involves technology with "feedback" capabilities and constitutes what is generally considered to be automated technology. In brief, as automaticity increases, the initiating control source moves from man to technology. The type of machine response is increasingly one in which the technology responds independently of man's actions.

A second distinguishing characteristic of automated technology is the integration of the various operations performed in the production process. Mechanization, according to Bright,[4] has at least three fundamental dimensions: level, span, and penetration. Level of mechanization, just discussed in terms of control, refers to the degree to which the machinery itself responds to environmental conditions. By span is meant the extent to which a series of production events are mechanized, that is, the degree to which the total sequence of the production process is performed by the technology. Penetration applies to the degree to which secondary activities in the production process are performed by the machinery. The greater the span of mechanization over the total production process and the greater the degree to which secondary functions are performed by the technology, the greater the degree of integration in the production system.

A leading proponent of automation as a revolutionary change, John Diebold, argues that automation is not merely a more sophisticated level of mechanization but "marks a breakthrough with past trends, a qualitative departure from the more conventional advance of technology that began with jagged pieces of flint and progressed up to the steam engine." [5] Diebold suggests

4. Bright, "Does Automation Raise Skill Requirements?" p. 88.
5. Diebold, *Automation: The Advent of the Automatic Factory*, p. 2.

that confusion over whether automated technology represents an evolutionary or a revolutionary process stems from emphasis on the machines associated with automation. Automation, he contends, is more than electronic computers, transfer machines, numerical tool controls, and oil refining instrument panels. Heretofore technological improvements have still left room for direct human intervention and control. Automation, based on the principle of feedback, institutes a new type of technology that controls its own operations. Concerns for human limitations in the design of machines can be put aside.

A second distinctive feature of automated technology, according to Diebold, is the obsolescence of the concept of discrete machines. An automated production system introduces an integrated system for manufacturing or information processing. For all his concern with automation as a revolutionary departure, Diebold's description of automation does not seem to differ significantly from that of Bright. They both see control and integration as characteristic of the most highly developed technological systems.

There is a way out of what may be only a semantic tangle. Most discussions of technology, Faunce points out, err in considering technology as a unitary phenomenon. Technological development should be conceived "as a sequence of changes in separate production components that form developmental stages characterized by different types of man-machine relationships." [6] Faunce divides production into four components, each of which is accomplished with one or four types of technologies. *Power technology* refers to energy sources in production. Tools and technology used in

---

6. William A. Faunce, "Automation and the Division of Labor," *Social Problems,* 13 (Fall 1965), p. 150.

production from raw materials constitute *processing technology*. The transfer of materials between processing operations involves *materials-handling technology*. *Control technology* regulates the quality and quantity of production.

According to Faunce, technological development in many industries reveals the following pattern of change in technological components: a substitution of inanimate for animate power encourages change first in processing, next in materials handling, and finally in production control. Of course, this series of changes in power technology, processing technology, materials-handling technology, and control technology does not follow this neat sequence of events for all industries. For example, some industries such as oil refining, chemical plants, and power plants had a highly developed materials-handling and control technology almost from the beginning. Other industries may not advance beyond highly developed processing technology.

In order to relate these four technological components to historical stages of technological development, it must be noted that "while technological development may occur independently in any one of the production components, a certain level of development of each is a necessary condition for further development of the others." [7] For example, it would have been fruitless to set up transfer technology in the production of automobile engine blocks until various processing operations like boring and milling had been sufficiently refined. Similarly, control devices could not be applied to this production process until adequate transfer technology was designed and operative.

Faunce links this sequence of development to three stages in the evolution of production technology which

---

7. *Ibid.,* p. 151.

can be found in most industries. The craft stage occurs prior to the mechanization of the four production components. In this stage the power source is animate, tools and simple machines are used in processing, and materials handling and control functions are performed manually. Many types of craftsmen come to mind on the blue-collar side, ranging from skilled artisans in small shops making handcrafted products to journeymen performing maintenance and engineering functions in large factories. In the office, the craft period encompasses clerical work that requires only paper and a pencil, as well as jobs involving intermittent use of machines such as typewriters and adding machines.

Mechanized production, the second stage, involves development of inanimate power technology and mechanical processing technology. This is evident in the factory system where electrically driven tools and machines are applied by special-purpose machine operators in the completion of small parts of the total production process. The most frequently cited example is the assembly-line worker utilizing a power tool on a particular segment of automobiles as they are transported down the line. This type of mass production is not as prevalent as the myriad of non-assembly-line machine-operating jobs in the factory. In this stage materials-handling procedures are in the early stages of mechanization, and control is manually exercised.[8]

Punched-card data processing ushered into the office a type of mechanization analogous to that experienced in the factory. Tasks formerly done by hand can be processed through each of the special-purpose machines upon which this system of data processing is predicated. Materials-handling technology is not highly developed.

---

8. Control of quantity is somewhat automatic in the case of the assembly line since the speed of the line can be varied.

At each special-purpose machine, cards must be manually entered and removed by the operator. Control largely resides in the operator who wires the board instructing the machine and initiates each machine run.

The last stage, automated technology, takes its characteristic form in highly developed materials-handling technology and in the use of automatic production control. In the automated stage materials-handling technology and control technology may take one of several forms.[9] So-called Detroit automation or transfer technology involves conveyors that transport, for example, an engine block, from one automatic processing machine to the next. Except for maintenance stops, the production process is a continuous one, achieved with almost no direct human labor. Technology in chemical and petroleum processing is more highly developed in terms of integration (automatic materials handling) and automatic control. In petroleum refining, for example, crude oil derivatives are automatically transported from one processing unit to another. Petroleum derivatives, from their introduction as undifferentiated crude oil until their release into transportation vehicles, are not touched by human hands. Control is accomplished by feedback mechanisms that regulate such essentials as temperature and pressure.

Computerization in the office permits the integration of a multitude of formerly discrete clerical functions.[10]

---

9. Various types of automation are more fully discussed in Edgar Weinberg, "A Review of Automatic Technology," *Monthly Labor Review,* 78 (June 1955), pp. 637–644; and Louis E. Davis, "The Effects of Automation on Job Design," *Industrial Relations,* 11 (October 1962), pp. 53–71.

10. An electronic data-processing executive interviewed in connection with the present study stated that prior to integration through computerization a single insurance policy may have required forty punch cards scattered at various places throughout

Once the program, other operating instructions, and data on which operations are to be performed are entered into the computer's "memory," data are automatically transferred from one processing step to the next. Instructions entered into the computer control its operations on the data automatically until the processing job is completed.

Materials handling and control are performed automatically in transfer, continuous-process, and electronic data-processing types of automated technology. For that reason, the job responsibilities of operators in each type of automation are not primarily of a manual nature. Requirements of vigilance to detect malfunction in these systems means that they primarily perform a monitoring function.

Faunce's conception of automation emphasizes automatic control and integration, the same distinctive features underlined by Bright and Diebold. The definition of automation as applied to manufacturing or data processing as a highly integrated production system that is technologically controlled includes these two essential characteristics differentiating automation from mechanization.

A compelling argument for the evolutionary conception of automation is that materials-handling technology and control technology may be quite rudimentary, as in certain manufacturing industries and in punched-card systems in the office. Or materials handling and control technology may be highly developed, as in the production of chemicals, and moderately developed, as in the utilization of computers in some white-collar industries. The level of development of these compo-

---

the company. Today master files are contained in storage devices (tapes, data cells, disc drives). And with random-access capabilities all information on a policy can be obtained quite rapidly.

nents of technology are a matter of degree.

As Faunce notes, failure to recognize this has resulted in a variety of levels of technological development being described as automation. One consequence is that studies of automation often seem to reveal contradictory results. For example, Walker's study of a semi-automatic steel tube manufacturing plant[11] and Faunce's study of a semiautomatic automobile factory[12] did not find a feeling among workers that they had an increase in responsibility in their new jobs. On the other hand, studies by Blauner[13] and Mann and Hoffman,[14] conducted in industries with more highly developed materials handling and control technology, found that workers in their new automated jobs did experience an increase in responsibility. And in the office, Hoos's[15] findings are often generalized to computerized work settings, when in fact they apply to the stage of office mechanization known as the punched-card system of data processing. Confusion over the impact of automation stems partly from a failure to distinguish between the levels of development in the materials handling and control components of production technology.

The debate as to the evolutionary or revolutionary character of automated technology seems to be somewhat academic and partially due to a lack of perspective.

---

11. Charles R. Walker, *Toward the Automatic Factory: A Case Study of Men and Machines* (New Haven: Yale University Press, 1957).
12. William A. Faunce, "Automation in the Automobile Industry: Some Consequences for In-Plant Social Structure," *American Sociological Review,* 23 (August 1958), pp. 401–409.
13. Robert Blauner, *Alienation and Freedom* (Chicago: University of Chicago Press, 1964).
14. Floyd C. Mann and L. Richard Hoffman, *Automation and the Worker* (New York: Henry Holt, 1960).
15. Ida R. Hoos, *Automation in the Office* (Washington, D.C.: Public Affairs Press, 1961).

Henry Ford's assembly line, considered to be a revolutionary technological change, was built on previous technological knowledge organized in a new and unique fashion. It seems that each major advance in production technology is in its time considered revolutionary but, with the passage of time, can in retrospect be viewed as part of an evolutionary process. What is revolutionary yesterday is evolutionary today.

Bibliography

Aiken, Michael, and Hage, Jerald. "Organizational Alienation: A Comparative Analysis." *American Sociological Review*, 31 (August 1966):497–507.

"Automation." *The Annals of the American Academy of Political and Social Science*, 340 (March 1962):192 pp.

Bell, Daniel. "Adjusting Men to Machines." *Commentary*, 3 (January 1947):79–88.

Bendix, Reinhard. *Work and Authority in Industry* (New York: Harper & Row, Publishers, 1963).

Blauner, Robert. "Work Satisfaction and Industrial Trends in Modern Society." In *Labor and Trade Unionism*. Edited by Walter Galenson and Seymour Martin Lipset (New York: John Wiley & Sons, 1960), pp. 339–360.

Blauner, Robert. *Alienation and Freedom; The Factory Worker and His Industry* (Chicago: University of Chicago Press, 1964).

Blum, Albert. "Computers and Clerical Workers." Oberhausen, Germany: Document of the Third International Conference on Rationalization, Automation and Technological Change, sponsored by the Metal Workers' Industrial Union of the Federal Republic of Germany, 1968.

Bright, James R. *Automation and Management* (Boston: Division of Research, Graduate School of Business Administration, Harvard University, 1958).

Bright, James R. "Does Automation Raise Skill Requirements?" *Harvard Business Review*, 36 (July–August 1958): 85–99.

Broom, Leonard, and Selznick, Philip. *Sociology*, 4th edition (New York: Harper & Row, Publishers, Inc., 1968).

Browning, Charles, et al. "On the Meaning of Alienation." *American Sociological Review*, 26 (October 1961):780–781.

Buckingham, Walter. *Automation: Its Impact on Business and People* (New York: The New American Library, 1963).

Centers, Richard. "Motivational Aspects of Occupational Stratification." *Journal of Social Psychology*, 28 (November 1948):187–217.

Chinoy, Ely. *Automobile Workers and the American Dream* (Garden City: Doubleday & Company, Inc., 1955).

Clark, John P. "Measuring Alienation Within a Social System." *American Sociological Review,* 24 (December 1959): 849–852.

Craig, Harold F. *Administering a Conversion to Electronic Accounting* (Boston: Division of Research, Graduate School of Business Administration, Harvard University, 1955).

Crossman, E. R. F. W. *Automation and Skill* (London: Her Majesty's Stationery Office, 1960).

Dale, J. R. *The Clerk in Industry* (Liverpool University Press, 1962).

Davis, Louis E. "Job Design and Productivity: A New Approach." *Personnel,* 33 (March 1957):418–430.

Davis, Louis E. "The Effects of Automation on Job Design." *Industrial Relations,* 11 (October 1962):53–71.

Davis, Louis E. "The Design of Jobs." *Industrial Relations,* 6 (October 1966):21–45.

Davis, Louis E., and Werling, Richard. "Job Design Factors." *Occupational Psychology,* 34 (April 1960):109–132.

Dean, Dwight G. "Alienation: Its Meaning and Measurement." *American Sociological Review,* 26 (October 1961): 755–758.

DeBivort, H. "Automation—Some Social Aspects." *International Labour Review,* 72 (December 1955):466–495.

Delehanty, George E. "Office Automation and Occupation Structure: A Case Study of Five Insurance Companies." *Industrial Management Review,* 7 (Spring 1966):99–108.

Diebold, John. *Automation: The Advent of the Automatic Factory* (New York: D. Van Nostrand Co., Inc., 1952).

Diebold, John. *Criteria and Bases for a Study on the Extent of Automation in American Industry,* Manpower Administration of U.S. Department of Labor, Office of Manpower, Automation and Training, January 1964.

Dubin, Robert. "Industrial Workers' Worlds: A Study of the 'Central Life Interests' of Industrial Workers." *Social Problems,* 3 (January 1956):131–142.

Durkheim, Emile. *The Division of Labor in Society* (Glencoe, Illinois: The Free Press, 1964).

"Effects of Mechanisation and Automation in Offices: I." *International Labour Review*, 81 (February 1960):154–173.

"Effects of Mechanisation and Automation in Offices: II." *International Labour Review*, 81 (March 1960):255–273.

"Effects of Mechanisation and Automation in Offices: III." *International Labour Review*, 81 (April 1960):350–369.

Elliott, J. Douglas. "Increasing Office Productivity Through Job Enlargement." In *The Human Side of the Office Manager's Job*, 134, Office Management Series: American Management Association, 1953.

Faunce, William A. "Automation in the Automobile Industry: Some Consequences for In-Plant Social Structure." *American Sociological Review*, 23 (August 1958):401–407.

Faunce, William A. "The Automobile Industry: A Case Study in Automation." *Automation and Society*. Edited by Howard Boone Jacobson and Joseph S. Roucek (New York: Philosophical Library, Inc., 1959), pp. 44–53.

Faunce, William A. "Automation and the Division of Labor." *Social Problems*, 13 (Fall 1965):149–160.

Faunce, William A. *Problems of an Industrial Society* (New York: McGraw-Hill Book Company, 1968).

Faunce, William A., Hardin, Einar, and Jacobson, Eugene H. "Automation and the Employee." *The Annals of the American Academy of Political and Social Science*, 340 (March 1962):60–68.

Francois, William. *Automation: Industrialization Comes of Age* (New York: Collier Books, 1964).

Freeman, Audrey. "Office Automation in the Insurance Industry." *Monthly Labor Review*, 88 (November 1965): 1313–1319.

Friedmann, Georges. *Industrial Society* (Chicago: The Free Press, 1955).

Friedmann, Georges. *The Anatomy of Work* (New York: The Free Press of Glencoe, 1961).

Fueur, Lewis. "What Is Alienation? The Career of a Concept." In *Sociology on Trial*, edited by Maurice Stein and

Arthur Vidich (Englewood Cliffs, New Jersey: Prentice-Hall, 1963), pp. 127–147.

Ginsberg, Barry M. "The Impact of Automation on Wage and Salary Administration." *ILR Research,* 9 (1963):3–9.

Goldthorpe, John H. "Attitudes and Behavior of Car Assembly Workers: A Deviant Case and a Theoretical Critique." *British Journal of Sociology,* 17 (September 1966): 227–244.

Guest, Robert H. "Job Enlargement—A Revolution in Job Design." *Personnel Administration,* 20 (March–April 1957):9–16.

Hajda, Jon. "Alienation and Integration of Student Intellectuals." *American Sociological Review,* 26 (October 1961):758–777.

Hardin, Einar. "Computer Automation, Work Environment, and Employee Satisfaction: A Case Study." *Industrial and Labor Relations Review,* 13 (July 1960):557–567.

Hardin, Einar. "The Reactions of Employees to Office Automation." *Monthly Labor Review,* 83 (September 1960): 925–932.

Helfgott, Roy B. "EDP and the Office Work Force." *Industrial and Labor Relations Review,* 19 (July 1966):503–516.

Herzberg, Frederick, et al. *Job Attitudes: Review of Research and Opinion* (Pittsburgh: Psychological Service of Pittsburgh, 1957).

Hoos, Ida R. "The Impact of Office Automation on Workers." *International Labour Review,* 82 (1960):363–388.

Hoos, Ida R. "When the Computer Takes Over the Office." *Harvard Business Review,* 38 (July–August 1960):102–114.

Hoos, Ida R. *Automation in the Office* (Washington, D.C.: Public Affairs Press, 1961).

Hyman, Herbert H. "The Value Systems of Different Classes: A Social-Psychological Contribution to the Analysis of Stratification." In *Class, Status, and Power.* Edited by Reinhard Bendix and Seymour Lipset (Glencoe, Illinois: The Free Press, 1953), pp. 426–442.

Jacobson, Eugene, Trumbo, Don, Cheek, Gloria, and Nangle, John. "Employee Attitudes Toward Technological

Change in a Medium Sized Insurance Company." *Journal of Applied Psychology,* 43 (December 1959):349–354.

Jaffe, Abram J., and Froombin, Joseph. *Technology and Jobs: Automation in Perspective* (New York: F. A. Praeger, 1968).

Josephson, Eric, and Josephson, Mary (eds.). *Man Alone: Alienation in Modern Society* (New York: Dell Publishing Company, 1962).

Jurgensen, Clifford E. "Selected Factors Which Influence Job Preference." *Journal of Applied Psychology,* 31 (December 1947):553–564.

Kennedy, James E., and O'Neill, Harry E. "Job Content and Workers' Opinions." *Journal of Applied Psychology,* 42 (December 1958):372–375.

Kilbridge, Maurice D. "Turnover, Absence and Transfer Rates as Indicators of Employee Dissatisfaction With Repetitive Work." *Industrial and Labor Relations Review,* 15 (October 1961):21–32.

Krant, Allen. "How EDP Is Affecting Workers and Organizations." *Personnel,* 39 (July–August 1962):38–50.

Kushner, Albert. "People and Computers." *Personnel,* 40 (January–February 1963):27–34.

Lecky, Prescott. *Self-Consistency* (Hamden, Connecticut: The Shoe String Press, Inc., 1961).

Lee, H. C. "Do Workers Really Want More Flexibility on the Job?" *Personnel,* 42 (March–April 1965):74–77.

Lee, H. C. "Electronic Data Processing and Skill Requirements." *Personnel Administration,* 29 (May–June 1966): 50–53.

Lindahl, Lawrence G. "What Makes a Good Job." *Personnel,* 25 (January 1949):263–266.

Lipsteu, Otis, and Reed, Kenneth A. "Automation's Impact on Personnel Administration: A Case Study." *Personnel,* 42 (January–February 1965):40–49.

Lyman, Elizabeth. "Occupational Differences in the Value Attached to Work." *American Journal of Sociology,* 61 (September 1955):138–144.

MacKinney, A. C., et al. "Has Specialization Reduced Job Satisfaction?" *Personnel,* 39 (January–February 1962):8–17.

Mann, Floyd C., and Hoffman, L. Richard. "Individual and Organizational Correlates of Automation." *Journal of Social Issues,* 12 (1956):7–17.

Mann, Floyd C., and Hoffman, L. Richard. *Automation and the Worker* (New York: Henry Holt, 1960).

Mann, Floyd C., and Hoffman, L. Richard. "Psychological and Organizational Impacts." In *Automation and Technological Change.* Edited by John T. Dunlop (Englewood Cliffs, New Jersey: Prentice-Hall, Inc., 1962), pp. 43–65.

Mann, Floyd C., and Williams, Lawrence K. "Organizational Impact of White Collar Automation." *Annual Proceedings,* Industrial Relations Research Association, Madison, Wisconsin (December 1958):59–69.

Mann, Floyd C., and Williams, Lawrence K. "Observations on the Dynamics of a Change to Electronic Data Processing Equipment." *Administrative Science Quarterly,* 5 (September 1960):217–256.

Mann, Floyd C., and Williams, Lawrence K. "Some Effects of the Changing Work Environment in the Office." *Journal of Social Issues,* 18 (July 1962):90–101.

Marcson, Simon (ed.). *Automation, Alienation, and Anomie* (New York: Harper and Row, Publishers, 1970).

Marx, Karl. "Alienated Labor." *Man Alone: Alienation in Modern Society.* Edited by Eric Josephson and Mary Josephson (New York: Dell Publishing Company, 1962), pp. 93–105.

McGill Industrial Relations Centre Review, 2 (Spring 1968): 6–7.

Mead, George Herbert. *Mind, Self, and Society* (Chicago: University of Chicago Press, 1937).

Mills, C. Wright. *White Collar* (New York: Oxford University Press, 1956).

Morse, Nancy C., and Weiss, R. S. "The Function and Meaning of Work and the Job." *American Sociological Review,* 20 (April 1955):191–198.

Mumford, Enid, and Banks, Olive. *The Computer and the Clerk* (London: Routledge & Kegan Paul, 1967).

Murphy, Gardner. *Personality* (New York: Harper and Brothers, Publishers, 1947).

Neal, Arthur G., and Rettig, Salomon. "Dimensions of Alienation Among Manual and Non-Manual Workers." *American Sociological Review*, 28 (August 1963):599–608.

Neal, Arthur G., and Rettig, Salomon. "On the Multidimensionality of Alienation." *American Sociological Review*, 32 (February 1967):54–64.

Nettler, Gwynn. "A Measure of Alienation." *American Sociological Review*, 22 (December 1957):670–677.

"On-Site Systems Top 30,000 Mark." *Business Automation*, 13 (February 1966):54–56.

Orzack, Louis H. "Work as a 'Central Life Interest' of Professionals." *Social Problems*, 7 (Fall 1959):125–132.

Palmer, G. L. "Attitudes Toward Work in an Industrial Community." *American Journal of Sociology*, 63 (July 1957):17–26.

Pearlin, Leonard I. "Alienation from Work: A Study of Nursing Personnel." *American Sociological Review*, 27 (June 1962):314–326.

Porter, Lyman W. "A Study of Perceived Need Satisfaction in Bottom and Middle Management Jobs." *Journal of Applied Psychology*, 45 (February 1961):1–10.

Porter, Lyman W. "Job Attitudes in Management: I. Perceived Deficiencies in Need Fulfillment as a Function of Job Level." *Journal of Applied Psychology*, 46 (December 1962):375–384.

Rhee, H. A. *Office Automation in Social Perspective* (London: Basil Blackwell, 1968).

Rico, Leonard. "The Staffing Process and the Computer." *Management of Personnel Quarterly*, 1 (Autumn–Winter 1962):32–38.

Rico, Leonard. *The Advance Against Paperwork* (Ann Arbor, Michigan: Bureau of Industrial Relations, Graduate School of Business Administration, University of Michigan, 1967).

Roper, Elmo. "The Fortune Survey—The American Factory Worker: What's Good About His Job? . . . What's Bad About It?" *Fortune,* 35 (May 1947):5–12.

Seeman, Melvin. "On the Meaning of Alienation." *American Sociological Review,* 24 (December 1959):783–791.

Seeman, Melvin. "On the Personal Consequences of Alienation in Work." *American Sociological Review,* 32 (April 1967):273–285.

Shepard, Jon M. "Man-Machine Relationships, Attitudes Toward Work and Meanings in the Work Role." Unpublished Ph.D. Dissertation, Michigan State University, 1968.

Shepard, Jon M. "Functional Specialization and Work Attitudes." *Industrial Relations,* 8 (February 1969):185–194.

Shepard, Jon M. "Functional Specialization, Alienation and Job Satisfaction." *Industrial and Labor Relations Review,* 23 (January 1970):207–219.

Simmon, J. L. "Some Intercorrelations Among 'Alienation Measures.' " *Social Forces,* 44 (March 1966):370–372.

Sola, F. C. "Personnel Administration and Office Automation: A Review of Empirical Research." *ILR Research,* 8 (1962).

Stettner, Leonora. "Survey of Literature on Social and Economic Effects of Technical Change." In *Employment Problems of Automation and Advanced Technology: An International Perspective.* Edited by Jack Stieber (London: Macmillan, 1966).

Stieber, Jack. "Automation and the White-Collar Worker." *Personnel,* 34 (November–December 1957):8–17.

Struening, Elmer L., and Richardson, Arthur H. "A Factor Analytic Exploration of the Alienation, Anomia, and Authoritarianism Domain." *American Sociological Review,* 33 (October 1965):768–776.

Sultan, Paul E., and Prasow, Paul. "Automation: Some Classification and Measurement Problems." *Labor and Automation,* Bulletin No. 1, 1964.

Sultan, Paul, and Prasow, Paul. "The Skill Impact of Automation." *Exploring the Dimensions of the Manpower Revolution, Volume I of Selected Readings in Employment and*

Manpower. Compiled for the Subcommittee on Employment and Manpower of the Committee on Labor and Public Welfare, United States Senate, 1964.

Swados, Harvey. "The Myth of the Happy Worker." In *Man Alone: Alienation in Modern Society.* Edited by Eric Josephson and Mary Josephson (New York: Dell Publishing Company, 1962), pp. 106–113.

The Employment Impact of Technological Change. Appendix Vol. II, Technology and the American Economy, The Report of the National Commission on Technology, Automation, and Economic Progress, February 1966. Especially Part 3 "Skill Requirements," pp. 207–287, and "Changing Character of Human Work Under the Impact of Technological Change," pp. 293–315.

Turner, Arthur N., and Lawrence, Paul R. *Industrial Jobs and the Worker* (Boston: Division of Research, Graduate School of Business Administration, Harvard University, 1965).

U.S. Department of Labor, Bureau of Labor Statistics. *Studies on Automatic Technology: Number 2 — The Introduction of an Electronic Computer in a Large Insurance Company* (Washington, D.C.: U.S. Government Printing Office, 1955).

U.S. Department of Labor, Bureau of Labor Statistics. *A Case Study of a Large Mechanized Bakery* (Washington, D.C.: U.S. Government Printing Office, 1956).

U.S. Department of Labor, Bureau of Labor Statistics, Bulletin Number 1241. *Automation and Employment Opportunities for Office Workers* (Washington, D.C.: U.S. Government Printing Office, 1958).

U.S. Department of Labor, Bureau of Labor Statistics. *Adjustments to the Introduction of Office Automation* (Washington, D.C.: U.S. Government Printing Office, 1960).

U.S. Department of Labor, United States Civil Service Commission, *A Study of the Impact of Automation on Federal Employees* (Washington, D.C.: U.S. Government Printing Office, 1964).

U.S. Department of Labor, Bureau of Employment Security. *Occupations in Electronic Computing Systems* (Washington, D.C.: U.S. Government Printing Office, 1965).

U.S. Department of Labor, Bureau of Labor Statistics. *Technological Trends in Major American Industries* (Washington, D.C.: U.S. Government Printing Office, 1966).

U.S. Department of Labor, Bureau of Labor Statistics. *Impact of Office Automation in the Insurance Industry* (Washington, D.C.: U.S. Government Printing Office, 1966).

Van Auken, Jr., K. G. "A Case Study of the Impact of Automation on Skills and Equipment." In *Man and Automation,* The Technology Project (New Haven, Conn.: Yale University Press, 1956).

Walker, Charles R. "The Problem of the Repetitive Job." *Harvard Business Review,* 28 (May 1950):54–59.

Walker, Charles R. *Toward the Automatic Factory* (New Haven: Yale University Press, 1957).

Walker, Charles R., and Guest, Robert H. *The Man on the Assembly Line* (Cambridge: Harvard University Press, 1952).

Walker, J., and Marriott, R. "A Study of Some Attitudes to Factory Work." *Occupational Psychology,* 25 (July 1951): 181–191.

Weber, C. Edward. "Impact of Electronic Data Processing on Clerical Skills." *Personnel Administration,* 22–33 (January–February 1959):20–26.

Wedderburn, Dorothy. "Are White-Collar and Blue-Collar Jobs Converging? The Impact of Technology Upon Occupational-Structure and Content." Oberhausen, Germany: Document of the Third International Conference on Rationalization, Automation and Technological Change, sponsored by the Metal Workers' Industrial Union of the Federal Republic of Germany, 1968.

Weinberg, Edgar. "A Review of Automatic Technology." *Monthly Labor Review,* 78 (June 1955):637–644.

Weinberg, Edgar. "Experiences With the Introduction of Office Automation." *Monthly Labor Review,* 83 (April 1960):376–380.

Whisler, Thomas L., and Meyer, Harold. *The Impact of EDP on Life Company Organization* (New York: Life Office Management Association, Personnel Administration Report, 34, 1967).

Wiener, Rose. "Changing Manpower Requirements in Banking." *Monthly Labor Review,* 85 (September 1962): 989–995.

Wilensky, Harold L. "Varieties of Work Experience." In *Man in a World of Work.* Edited by Henry Borow (Boston: Houghton Mifflin Company, 1964).

Zetterberg, Hans L. "Compliant Actions." *Acta Sociologia,* 2 (1957):179–201.

Index

Ability, 57, 117. *See also* Skill requirements
Accounting-machine operators, 58
Accuracy, 46
Achievement, and relevant status criteria, 35–36
Adding machines, 43, 63
Addressograph operators, 108
Advancement, *see* Promotion
Age, 127
Alienation, 5, 6, 9, 40; and phases of man-machine relationship, 10, 20, 106–110; and division of labor, 12; definition and measurement of, 13–22; variants of, 13–17, 89–95; self-alienation, 15–16; of blue-collar workers, 21, 107; industrial workers, 23–40; and status structure, 36–39; impact of technology upon, 39–40; among clerical employees, 40, 62–95; among software personnel, 65–67, 73, 82–84; female-male comparisons, 73, 77, 82–86, 89, 103; factory worker-office worker comparisons, 96–106, 114–116; overview, 107–128; man-machine relationship in office, 108–114; ana functional specialization, 111; implications of findings on, 116–123; and third-generation computers, 122; industry variations, 123–124; scale construction, 129–135
Anomie, 15
Artisans, 108. *See also* Craftsmen
Assemblers, 24, 31, 40; and sense of powerlessness, 25, 100; and sense of meaninglessness, 29–30, 100; and self-evaluative involvement, 39, 84; compared to office machine operators, 103, 105, 114
Assembly line, 25, 140; automobile, 7, 20–22, 144
Attitudes: production personnel, 2–3; office workers, 5, 9; blue-

collar and white-collar compared, 101–106, 114; convergence of office workers' and factory workers', 114–116; and functional specialization, 116–117; and variables of job satisfaction, 126–128
Automated production systems, 7–8, 119. *See also* Production systems
Automation, 2, 6, 107–128; differentiated from mechanization, 5, 118, 136–144; and functional specialization, 23, 58, 118; and production processes, 30–31; relation to skill requirements, 55–56; and convergence of attitudes of office and factory workers, 114–118; and nature of work, 125; distinguishing characteristics of, Bright's concept, 136–137; Diebold's definition, 138; Faunce's concept, 138–140, 142; evolutionary conception of, 142–144
Automobile workers, 7, 20–22, 25–26, 32, 140, 144; skilled maintenance trades, 28, 108

Banks, 17–18, 20, 58; computers in, 45–46; posting function, 51–52
Banks, Olive, 81
Blauner, Robert, 5, 6, 24, 30, 123–124; and variables of job satisfaction, 126; and studies on increase in responsibility, 143
Blue-collar sector, 4, 6; and man-machine relationship, 9–10; impact of technology on, 12; compared to white-collar sector, 101–106; convergence of attitudes with white-collar sector, 114–116. *See also* Factory workers
Bright, James R., 55, 119; mechanization profile, 136–137, 142
Bureau of Labor Statistics, 48, 49, 57, 61, 120

Business machines, multifunction, 43

Census, U.S., 3
Centers, Richard, 102
Centralization, organizational, 96
Chinoy, Ely, 32, 34
Circle Oil refinery, 20, 21, 26; job classifications, 32; promotion at, 34
Clerical workers, 6, 8–9, 18; impact of mechanization and computers on, 12, 41–63 *passim*; effects of technology on alienation among, 40, 62–95, 103, 105; in computerized office, 41; changing nature of work of, 47–50; in nonmechanized jobs, 50, 54–55, 62, 64, 70, 93, 97, 111; upgrading of skills in edp-affected departments, 50–52, 111; upgrading of skills outside edp unit, 52; and software personnel, 61–62; and powerlessness, 68–74, 92, 97; and meaninglessness, 74–77, 92; and normlessness, 77–83, 92–93, 105; and occupational mobility, 80–81; and self-evaluative involvement, 84, 93, 105; compared to factory workers, 96–106; ranking of job aspects, 101; and instrumental work orientation, 105; and man-machine relationship, 108–114; and amount of freedom and control, 117
Coders, 50. *See also* Proof-encoding machines
Commitment, 36
Communication, on-the-job, 127
Computer operators, 9, 18, 50, 63; and division of labor, 56–60; upgrading of, 57–58; increase in demand for, 59; and salary structure, 61; and alienation, 65, 82, 92; and powerlessness factor, 70–73, 109, 115; amount of freedom and control, 71, 104, 105, 117; and normlessness, 82, 117; and self-

evaluative involvement, 84, 86, 117; and instrumental work orientation, 86, 117; in factory-office comparison, 100, 103–106; and man-machine relationship, 108–110; and meaninglessness factor, 115, 117–118; correction capacity, 119; growth in numbers of, 119–120; and third-generation computers, 122
Computers, 3, 105; in offices, 4, 45, 47, 63, 141–142; and change, 5; impact on clerical workers, 12, 17–20, 50–62; capabilities of, 45–46; accuracy of, 46; memory and storage capacity, 46; and human intervention, 46–47; and elimination of routine jobs, 48–49, 58–59; upgrading effect among nonmechanized office workers, 50–52, 68–69; and increased business volume, 69; and integration of production process, 119–120; and man-machine relationship, 125
Console operators, *see* Computer operators
Continuous-process technology, 26, 30, 84, 104, 106; in oil refinery, 31; factors relating to meaningfulness, 31–33, 117; and decrease in alienation, 118; and "Detroit automation," 141
Control, 13–14, 83, 91–92, 96; and craftsmen, 24–25, 103, 105; of work pace, 25–26; in continuous-process technology, 26–27; of machine monitors, 26–28; as status criteria, 37; and programmers and systems analysts, 65, 67–68; of nonmechanized clerical workers, 69–70; and computer operator, 71, 104, 105, 117; differences in male-female reactions, 73; and job satisfaction, 126; and automaticity, 136–137; and technology, 139, 141–142. *See also* Powerlessness
Control clerks, 50. *See also* Clerical workers

Craft production systems, 7, 140; and functional specialization, 23
Craftsmen, 23, 28–29, 31, 40, 96–100, 140; and perceived powerlessness, 24–25, 97, 115; and perceived meaninglessness, 29–30, 115; and normlessness, 34–35; and self-evaluative involvement, 38, 84; compared to white-collar personnel, 103, 105, 115
Craig, Harold F., 50
Cultural differences, 127

Danger, physical, 31
Data processing, see Electronic data processing; Nonelectronic data processing
Deadlines, 68, 70
"Debugging," 71
Delehanty, George E., 48
"Detroit" automation, 2, 141
Diebold, John, 136–138, 142
Downgrading, job, 48, 54–55, 57, 104
Dubin, Robert, 125–126
Durkheim, Emile, 15

Education, 80, 127. See also Skill requirements
Electronic data processing, 18, 20, 43, 45–47, 108; effect on job upgrading, 48–51; and functional consolidation and integration, 60; level of alienation, 109. See also Computers
Environment, occupational, 5, 127
Expansion, organizational, 96, 113

Factory workers, 20–23, 84; impact of technology on alienation among, 39–40; compared to office workers, 96–106; semiskilled, 104; and phases of man-machine relationship, 107–108. See also Blue-collar sector
Faunce, William A., 6, 35, 138–140, 142, 143
Federal Government, see Government, U.S.

Feedback, 119, 137, 138, 141
Females, 73, 77, 89; and normlessness, 82–83, 93; and self-evaluative involvement, 84–86, 94, 109–110; and powerlessness, 92; and instrumental work orientation, 94; in factory worker-office worker comparison, 100; and man-machine relationship, 109
First World War, 43
Flexowriting machines, 108
Ford, Henry, 144
Freedom, 13–14, 83, 91–92, 96; and craftsmen, 24–25, 103; and as-sembly-line worker, 25–26; in continuous-process technology, 26–27; and machine monitors, 26–27; as status criteria, 37; and software personnel, 65, 67–68; and nonmechanized clerical worker, 69–70; and computer operator, 71, 104, 105, 117; differences in male-female reactions, 73. See also Powerlessness
Friedmann, Georges, 2
Function, interdependence of, 67–68, 69

Government, U.S., 3–4, 58; Bureau of Labor Statistics, 48, 49, 57, 61, 120
Guest, Robert H., 7, 26, 127

Hardin, Einar, 81
Hardware personnel, see Computer operators
Helfgott, Roy B., 49
Herzberg, Frederick, 127
Hoffman, L. Richard, 143
Hoos, Ida R., 54, 55, 143

IBM, 4; 360 series, 59, 120
Industrial sociology, 123–124
Industrial workers, see Factory workers
Information technology, 3
Instrumental work orientation, 16, 35–39, 40, 86–88, 94; in factory

Instrumental work orientation (*continued*)
worker-office worker comparison, 97, 100, 104, 105, 114; in factory workers, 107; male-female differences, 109–110; and computer operators, 117; in scale construction, 130–131, 134–135
Insurance companies, 4, 17–20, 58–59; and functional integration, 59–60; and software personnel, 61; consolidation of company records, 121
Integration: functional, 8, 59–60, 137, 138; work group, 126; technological, 141–142
Interpersonal relationships, 127
Interrelationships, knowledge of, 37
Involvement, self-evaluative, 16–17, 35–39, 40, 83–88, 93; in comparison of factory worker and office worker, 97, 100, 105, 114, 115; in factory workers, 107; male-female differences, 109–110; computer operators, 117; in scale construction, 130–131, 133–134

Job aspects, ranking of, 101–102, 127
Job classification, 7–9, 31–32, 63–64; enlargement of, 7–8, 56, 111–112, 116; elimination of, 8, 48–50, 58–59, 80–81; upgrading of, 48–52, 57, 62, 111–112; downgrading of, 48, 54–55, 57, 104; and computer operator, 56–60, 111–112; and powerlessness in clerical workers, 68
Job content, 104–105, 124
Jurgensen, Clifford E., 101

Key-punch operators, 18, 50, 58, 108, 120–121

Labor, division of, 1–2, 6–7; in craft production systems, 7; differentiation and relation to technology, 9, 23; and alienation among office and factory workers, 12, 25; and perceived meaninglessness, 29–30; and continuous-process technology, 31; and upgrading effect among non-mechanized office workers, 50–52; and office mechanization, 52-56, 64; for computer operators and software personnel, 56–62, 64; between computer operators and programmers, 71
Labor market, 69, 70
Lawrence, Paul R., 127
Lee, H. C., 49, 69, 70
Leisure, 125–126
Lindahl, Lawrence G., 102

Machine monitors, *see* Monitors, machine
Machine operators, 23, 43–45, 64; male, 100; female, 100; compared to assemblers, 103–106, 114. *See also* Computer operators
Males, 73, 76–77, 89, 91; and normlessness, 82–83, 93; and self-evaluative involvement, 84–86, 94, 109–110; and powerlessness, 92; and instrumental work orientation, 94; machine operator, 100; and man-machine relationship, 109
Man-machine relationship, 10, 20, 25, 40, 89–91; and perceived powerlessness, 24–29, 38; and perceived meaninglessness, 29, 38; perceived normlessness, 33–35, 38; and self-evaluative involvement, 35–39; and instrumental work orientation, 35–39; in the office, 41, 47, 52–53, 56, 64, 108–114; and alienation in the office, 64–95, 103; and factory workers, 107–108; and convergence of attitudes of office and factory workers, 114–116; importance of, 123–125
Management, 61, 128
Mann, Floyd C., 51, 81, 143
Marx, Karl, 1, 13, 15; and "alienated laor," 23
Master files, 120–122

Materials handling, automatic, 119; technology, 139, 141–142
Meaninglessness, 14–15, 29–33, 37, 40; and assemblers, 29; among machine monitors, 32–33; among office workers, 74–77, 92; in factory worker-office worker comparison, 97, 100, 103; in factory workers, 107; among programmers, 109; male-female differences, 109, 110; computer operators, 117–118; in scale construction, 130, 131
Mechanization, 2–3, 6, 63, 107–128; differentiated from automation, 5, 118, 136–144; impact on clerical employees, 12, 48–52; and subdivision of labor, 30; of office work, 42–47, 52–56, 111–113; and self-evaluative involvement of workers, 86; and instrumental work orientation, 86; and semi-skilled workers, 105; and convergence of attitudes of factory and office workers, 114–116; fundamental dimensions of, 137
Mechanized production systems, 7, 40; and functional specialization, 23
Mental ability, see Ability
Mental attention, 7
Merit, 15, 34, 83, 92–93, 117; and status structure, 37; and occupational structure, 80–82
Meyer, Harold, 50
Microfilm machine operators, 108
Mills, C. Wright, 4, 96
Mobility, occupational, 15, 34–35, 37, 78, 80–81, 117
Monitors, machine, 23–24, 40, 60; and perceived powerlessness, 25, 100–101; and mechanical pacing, 26–27; and freedom, 27–28; level of meaninglessness, 32–33; and self-evaluative involvement, 38–39, 84; and factory worker-office worker comparison, 100, 103–104; compared to craftsmen, 108; compared to computer operators, 115

Movement, physical, 26–27, 54; among computer operators, 72
MTST operators, 108
Multiprocessing, 122–123
Mumford, Enid, 81

New York Times, 4
Nonelectronic data processing, 18, 20
Normlessness, 15, 33–35, 37, 40, 92–93; among craftsmen, 34–35; among office workers, 77–83; and mechanized specialization, 78–80; and occupational structure, 80–81; in factory worker-office worker comparisons, 97, 100, 103–104, 105; in factory workers, 107; differences in male-female attitudes toward, 109, 110; in scale construction, 130–133

Objectification, of labor, 1
"Occupational community," 126–127
Occupational structure, 77–78, 80–83; computer operators, 104, 120–121
Office workers, see Clerical workers; White-collar workers
Offices, 4–5, 6, 41–62, 63; computerized, 4, 45, 47, 63, 141–142; man-machine relationship in, 8–9, 108–114; craft stage, 41–42, 140; effects of punched-card data processing on, 44–45, 47; and electronic data processing, 45–47; and changing nature of clerical work, 47–50; and division of labor, 50–62; alienation in, 62–95; powerlessness, 64–74; meaninglessness, 74–77; self-evaluative involvement of workers, 84; compared to factories, 96
Oil refinery, 31, 100, 141. See also Circle Oil Refinery
Organization: centralization of, 96; expansion of, 96, 113
Orientation, work, 15–17. See also Instrumental work orientation

Pacing, work, 7, 25–27, 68, 70; on assembly line, 25–26; of monitors, 26–27; in office, 63
Participation, in status structure, 36
Penetration, mechanization, 137
Petroleum refining, *see* Oil refinery
Posting, bank, 51–52
Power technology, 138–140
Powerlessness, 13–14, 37, 38, 40, 91–92; of factory workers 24–29, 107–108; of office workers, 64–74, 109; for software personnel, 67–68, 70–73, 92; for males, 73–74, 109; for females, 73–74, 109; of craftsmen, 97; in office worker-factory worker comparison, 97, 100, 105, 115; and third-generation computers, 122; in scale construction, 130–131
Prestige, occupational, 126. *See also* Status criteria
Procedures, work, 26
Processing technology, 139; mechanical, 140
Production systems, 107; craft, 7, 23, 140; and automation, 7–8, 30–31, 119–120; and mechanization, 7, 23, 40, 140; and technology, 24, 123, 139–140; control, 141
Programmers, 9, 18, 50, 57, 59, 60–61, 63; and division of labor, 64; and level of freedom and control, 65; level of alienation, 67, 109, 115; meaninglessness factor, 76; and normlessness, 82; and self-evaluative involvement, 84; and instrumental work orientation, 86; man-machine relationship, 109. *See also* Software personnel
Promotion, 32, 33, 101, 127; and merit, 34, 80–82
Proof-encoding machines, 108
Punched-card data processing, 43–45, 47, 52–53, 63, 64; decline in, 121; and office mechanization, 140–142

Repetitiveness, 7; in factory, 25, 31; in office, 52–53, 55, 58, 63
Responsibility, job, 48, 51–52, 57; of computer operator, 60, 111–112, 142; and automation, 143
Rewards, 15–16; economic, 102
Rico, Leonard, 48, 50
Role, and goals of organization, 14–15

Salary structure, 57, 61, 127
Sales workers, 101
Satisfaction, employee, 5, 102, 126–128
Security, 101, 102, 127
Seeman, Melvin, 13, 15–16
Self-alienation, 15–16. *See also* Alienation
Self-esteem, 17, 35–36, 125
Self-estrangement, 15–16
Self-evaluation, 35–36, 40. *See also* Involvement, self-evaluative
Separation, social-psychological, 96
Sex, *see* Females; Males
Skill requirements, 7, 43, 45, 63, 80; upgraded in edp-affected departments, 50–52, 111; reduction in, 55–56; of computer operators, 56–60; of software personnel, 61, 62
Sloan School of Management, M.I.T., 18, 22
Social interaction, 26, 54
Social psychology, 35
Social situations, 35
Sociology, industrial, *see* Industrial sociology
Software personnel, 59–62; level of alienation, 65–67, 92, 103, 105, 118; and powerlessness, 67–68, 70–73, 92, 101; and meaninglessness, 76, 92; and normlessness, 83, 93; and self-evaluative inolvement, 84; and instrumental work orientation, 86; in factory worker-office worker comparison, 100–101, 105; man-machine relationship, 109; male-female comparisons, 110; compared to craftsmen,

Softwear personnel (*continued*)
115; compared to oil refinery
monitors, 115. *See also* Programmers; Systems analysts
Sola, F. C., 56
Span, mechanization, 137
Specialization, functional, 1–2, 34,
69, 96; among office workers, 5, 44,
47–48, 52–56, 63–64, 112–113; and
technology, 6–9, 57–58, 118; and
mechanization, 23, 112–113;
among factory workers, 25; craft,
28; of nonmechanized clerks, 64,
113–114; and meaninglessness
among office workers, 74–77; and
normlessness, 78–80; and man-
machine relationship, 107, 111–
112; impact on work attitudes,
116–117, 126–128; increase in
office, 118–119
Standardization, 96
Status criteria, 17, 35–37, 101; and
alienation, 37–38
Stenographers, 20, 108
Supervision, 68, 70, 72, 127
Systems analysts, 9, 18, 50, 57, 59–
61, 63; and division of labor, 64;
and level of freedom and control,
65; and level of alienation, 67,
109, 115; meaninglessness factor,
76; normlessness factor, 82; and
self-evaluative involvement, 84;
and instrumental work orientation, 86; and man-machine relationship, 109. *See also* Software
personnel

Technology, 6, 96; and functional
specialization, 6–9, 57–58, 118;
and factory (industrial) workers,
12, 23–40; and office workers, 12,
50–56; continuous-process, 26, 30–
33, 84, 104, 106, 117, 118, 141;
and alienation, 39–40; and changing nature of clerical work, 47–
50; and attitudes of factory
worker and office worker, 114–116,
124; industry variations, 123, 124;
Faunce's view, 138–140; control,

139, 141–142; mechanized, 140–
141; automated, 141
Time-sharing, 122
Tools and technique, 7, 25
Transfer technology, *see* "Detroit"
automation
Turner, Arthur N., 127
Typists, 108
Typewriters, 43, 63, 140

UAW (United Automobile Work-
ers), 20–21
Unions, trade, 20, 127
U.S. Government, *see* Government,
U.S.
Upgrading, job, 48–52, 57, 62, 111–
112
Upward mobility, *see* Mobility

Wages, *see* Salary structure
Walker, Charles R., 7, 26, 127, 143
Weber, C. Edward, 54–55
Wedderburn, Dorothy, 104–105
Whisler, Thomas L., 50
White-collar workers, 4, 6, 22; and
man-machine relationship, 9–10;
impact of technology on, 12;
growth in employment, 69; as
Mills's "new proletariat," 96–97;
compared to blue-collar workers,
101–106; convergence of atti-
tudes with blue-collar sector, 114–
116. *See also* Clerical workers;
Offices
Williams, Lawrence K., 51, 81
Work group, 127
Working conditions, *see* Environ-
ment, occupational
World War I, *see* First World War
World War II, 3
Worth, personal, *see* Self-esteem